# The Great Bible Adventure

## Stories of well-known Bible people and events

Written by **Jill Gupta**

Illustrated by **Mychailo Kazybrid**

**CANDLE BOOKS**
GRAND RAPIDS, MICHIGAN

*To Tabitha*

*Love & prayers,*

*Grandpa Paul & Grandma Terry*

*2005*

Copyright © 2001 Angus Hudson Ltd
Text and cartoon illustrations copyright © Jill Gupta 1999

All rights reserved. No part of this publication may be reproduced, or
transmitted in any form or by any means, electronic or mechanical,
including photocopy, recording, or any information storage and retrieval
system, without permission in writing from the publisher.

Designed by Gazelle Creative Productions Ltd,
Concorde House, Grenville Place, Mill Hill, London NW7 3SA

Worldwide co-edition organized and produced by Angus Hudson Ltd,
Concorde House, Grenville Place, Mill Hill, London NW7 3SA
Tel: +44 208 959 3668 Fax: +44 208 959 3678

Published in the USA by Candle Books 2001
Distributed by Kregel Publications, PO Box 2607,
Grand Rapids, Michigan 49501

ISBN 0 8254 7218 0

Printed in Singapore

# Contents

# FACTS AND FIGURES

About four thousand years ago Abraham set out into the unknown. It seemed risky but he trusted God who'd promised that his people would become a great nation. Abraham's faith in God was tested—a test which involved his young son, Isaac.

Isaac's family was torn apart by favoritism and jealousy and his son Jacob repeated the mistake by making one of his twelve sons, Joseph, his favorite.

Joseph's brothers hated him and grabbed the opportunity to pack him off to Egypt. They joined him years later when Joseph was Governor, with plenty of food at his disposal, and they were suffering from famine. They settled in Egypt happily but three hundred years later, the Egyptians turned against the foreigners living in their country and made them slaves. The baby boys born to the slaves were killed but Moses escaped. His mother hid him in a basket on the River Nile. The Pharaoh's daughter found him and adopted him. He fled from Egypt after killing an Egyptian taskmaster but later returned to lead his people into the Promised Land.

The Israelites wandered in the desert for forty years before invading the Promised Land. Led by judges they settled down alongside the native population in Palestine. There were frequent clashes with enemies such as the Philistines. Some battles were lost and some were won, but they stayed put. Their most important city was Shiloh. Samuel grew up there with Eli the priest.

Samuel anointed Saul the first king of Israel after the Israelites decided they must have a monarchy. He was a failure but David who succeeded him was a roaring success. He united the people, defeated their enemies and made Jerusalem the capital city. His son, Solomon, built the Temple in Jerusalem but, soon after Solomon's death, the kingdom divided into two,

Israel in the north and Judah in the south.

Many Canaanites lived in Israel and Judah. Some Israelites started worshiping the Canaanite god, Baal. Prophets like Elijah put their lives on the line by condemning false gods and reminding the people that there was only one true God. After two hundred years the Assyrians destroyed the northern kingdom. In 587 B.C. the Babylonians destroyed Jerusalem and took the people into exile. Daniel was among the exiles. Not even a bunch of hungry lions would stop him staying true to God.

The Persians defeated the Babylonians in 539 B.C. and allowed the Jews to return to Jerusalem. They rebuilt the Temple and the city. In Persia, a Jewish girl, Esther, married King Xerxes I. She saved her fellow Jews from being massacred.

Throughout the hard times during and after the Exile, the Jews kept hoping that God would send his Messiah who would bring freedom, peace and prosperity.

# A Moving Story

Abraham looked up at the stars which spangled the night sky. He was excited and worried, all at the same time. He was leaving his home and he had no idea where he was going! He just knew that God wanted him to leave Haran. Abraham wasn't a young man and people thought he was taking a tremendous risk, but he reckoned God would guide him to where he wanted him to go. All his neighbors and friends turned out to watch as Abraham, his wife Sarah and his nephew Lot, his family and all their cattle, sheep, goats and servants, left

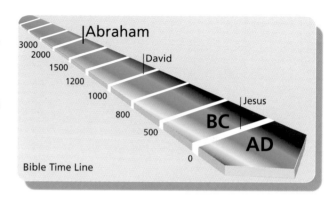

Haran to start their journey into the unknown.

The novelty of this extraordinary expedition soon wore off. Abraham and Lot's servants settled into a daily routine of fighting over whose animals should graze on what little grass remained around their camp. Abraham had to be practical. There were just too many of them to move around the country in one unit. He decided they must split up, so he gave Lot first choice of where to settle. Lot had an eye for the main chance and, without a moment's hesitation, he chose the beautiful, fertile Jordan Valley. Lot left his uncle, and with

CAN'T GET THE CAMELS INTO THE PACKING CASES, BOSS!!

THIS WAY UP

ABRAHAM'S GRASS!

LOT'S GRASS!

THEY'RE JUST ANIMALS!!

his wife, daughters and servants went to live just outside the city of Sodom. He didn't realize that he was leading his family into extreme danger.

Abraham was really tuned into God. He knew that Sodom was an evil place and God was going to destroy it. He pleaded with God to save the city in case there were any good people still living there. But Lot was the only good man in the city and he was in real trouble.

A huge crowd of men were besieging Lot's house. Lot had two guests staying with him and the men demanded he send them out. Lot knew they'd be unlikely to survive if he gave in to the mob. He had to escape from Sodom but he was delayed by his daughters' fiancés. They wouldn't hurry up because they thought Lot was joking. In the end, Lot had to leave them behind as he, his wife and daughters ran for their lives. As they reached safety, roaring fires swept through the cities of Sodom and Gomorrah, totally destroying them. Lot and his daughters were safe, but his wife made the mistake of turning to look back at the burning cities. It was the last thing she ever did.

You can read the full story in Genesis 12, 13, 19

# A Testing Time

Isaac was tied hand and foot. The bundles of wood he lay on dug into him and he could smell the smoke from the coals burning in a container

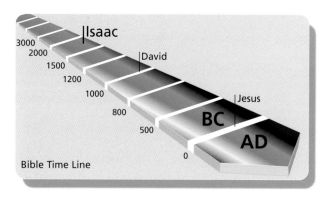

Bible Time Line

prepare an altar. It felt good to be treated like an adult. They found a flat stone on which they arranged the dry wood they had brought with them from home. Isaac wondered why they hadn't brought a lamb with them, but his father assured him that God would provide a sacrifice.

Isaac was taken completely by surprise. His father had moved swiftly and surely, tying his hands and feet and lifting him carefully but firmly on to the pile of wood. Stretched out on the altar,

on the ground nearby. He stared up at his father, Abraham, who stood over him, holding a knife to his throat.

Only a few days ago he had been really excited. He and his father were going on a long journey to a mountainside to make a sacrifice to God. The journey had taken three days but at last they reached their destination. Isaac was pleased when Abraham asked him to help

I WASHED MY HORNS THIS MORNING AND I CAN'T DO A THING WITH THEM!

Isaac realized that he was the sacrifice. He was going to die. His father loved him deeply but he was going to kill him and burn his body to ashes!

Isaac braced himself for the downward sweep of the knife, but at that moment the angel of the Lord spoke to Abraham. God did not want him to sacrifice Isaac. The very fact that he had been willing to do it had proved beyond all possible doubt that he put God first in his life. Abraham dropped the knife. It clattered to the ground. Gently, he untied the ropes that held his son and helped him off the altar. A yard or two from where they stood, a ram was struggling to disentangle its horns from a bush. Abraham seized the ram, then he and Isaac sacrificed it to God. Afterwards they returned home to Beersheba. Isaac often thought about what had happened that day and how it had helped him to understand his father better and to feel even closer to God.

You can read the full story in Genesis 22

# Looking for Love

Abraham's chief servant was under real pressure to succeed. He'd promised his master he'd find a suitable bride for Isaac. Now he had to travel back to the place where Abraham came from and choose a suitable girl. He was worried about how he'd select her, how he'd manage to meet her parents and get their permission and then, the worst scenario, what if he found the right girl and she didn't want to go? As he traveled to northern Mesopotamia he prayed long and hard. At last, after a long journey, he reached a city where he stopped by a well. He knew that plenty of young girls would come to the well to draw water during the afternoon. As he waited with his ten, thirsty camels for them to arrive, he thought of a foolproof selection test.

Rebecca picked up her water jar and joined the other young women at the well. It was a hot afternoon and she felt sorry for the traveler who approached her. He asked for a drink and she was pleased to give him one. Seeing his camels kneeling down a few yards away, Rebecca offered to bring them water too and she made many journeys to and from the well until they had all been watered. Unwittingly, Rebecca had

AN INTENSE RELATIONSHIP!

passed the selection process with flying colors. She had proved what a kind, hospitable and caring woman she was—just perfect for Isaac!

The chief servant's heart was beating fast. Everything was going so well. It was time to take the next vital step. He clothes and masses of gold and silver jewelry—gifts for her in-laws-to-be, Rebecca set off with Abraham's servant. On the journey she had plenty of time to think about her new husband and life as a married woman. It was exciting and scary. Isaac felt the same. He

ONLY ANOTHER THIRTY-NINE GALLONS TO GO!!

ON A HOT DAY, A LARGE THIRSTY CAMEL CAN DRINK 42 GALLONS OF WATER!

asked Rebecca whether he could spend the night in her father's house. Rebecca assured him there was plenty of room and raced home to tell her mother. Rebecca's parents welcomed him into their home. He explained who his master was, what he had asked him to do and how he'd chosen Rebecca. He needn't have worried. Rebecca's father gladly agreed that she should return to Canaan and become Isaac's wife.

Next day, loaded down with new

couldn't stand the wait at home so he decided to travel part way to meet them. One evening, as he paced the fields impatiently, he saw a line of camels approaching. When they drew near, Rebecca dismounted. They looked at one another. It was love at first sight!

You can read the full story in Genesis 24

# Double Trouble

Jacob stirred the pot of lentil soup he was heating, but his mind was elsewhere. For as long as he could remember he had been obsessed by the unfairness of life. A matter of minutes had condemned him to a bleak future of nothingness, as he saw it, while his 'older' twin brother, Esau, got all the rights and privileges of the first-born son.

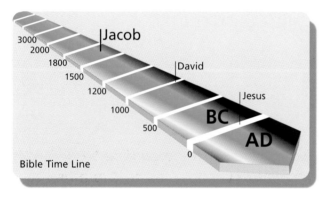

In the first place, Jacob didn't even like his brother. They had nothing in common. Esau was a macho man, always out hunting. His dad thought the world of him. Jacob preferred to be at home with his mom. Resentment and bitterness were messing up Jacob's life. All his energy was spent scheming to change things. Then it all fell into his lap without him having to make any effort at all. Esau handed over his rights as the first-born son without hesitation or argument. In fact he was eager to do so.

Esau was returning from a hunting trip. He was absolutely famished, and there was Jacob cooking some delicious soup. Esau begged for a bowlful. Jacob, seeing Esau was on the verge of collapse, calmly agreed but in exchange he wanted Esau's rights as the first-born son. Jacob was halfway there. But there was still the matter of the final blessing, given by a father to his son when he knew his death was near.

By now Isaac was old and blind. He realized he wasn't going to live much longer. Isaac decided to give his final blessing to Esau alone after he'd prepared him a tasty meal. But first Esau had to hunt down the main ingredient of the dish! Jacob would have missed out completely if his mom hadn't overheard Isaac talking to Esau.

Jacob was stunned when his mom told him what was going on. He was even more amazed by her plan for him to get the blessing instead. But Jacob

wasn't sure her plan would work. Getting Esau's birthrights had been easy. This time, though, he was going to have to impersonate his brother and he didn't sound, smell, or look the same as him. Sure, his dad couldn't see him but he could touch him. Esau was a barber's nightmare whereas Jacob was smooth-skinned. He'd never get away with it, but his mom would not be put off.

Rebecca cooked a meal of stewed goat and gave it to Jacob. Jacob draped himself in the goat's skin and took the food to his father, feeling very anxious and very hairy.

Despite sensing that something wasn't quite right, Isaac gave Jacob the final blessing thinking he was Esau.

Jacob didn't have much time to celebrate his success with his mom. Esau soon arrived home and discovered that Jacob had cheated him again. He vowed he would kill him. Jacob took the threat seriously and fled to his uncle's in Haran, hoping things would cool down after a while. They didn't and he never saw his mom again.

You can read the full story in Genesis 25, 27

# Arranged Marriages

Jacob had been on an emotional roller-coaster since running away from home. Terrified that Esau was going to catch up with him and kill him, he'd also felt lonely and homesick on the journey to his uncle Laban's. It was a great relief to arrive in one piece but before he had time to settle down in his new life he'd fallen head over heels in love with Laban's younger daughter, Rachel. But unfortunately he'd come empty-handed which didn't do much for his chances of marrying her. Still, he'd worked hard for his uncle without pay ever since his arrival, and

You can read the full story in Genesis 29, 30

when Laban insisted on paying him, Jacob realized he'd got something to bargain with.

Laban was pleased with his nephew. He'd fitted into the family well, worked hard and treated his daughters with respect. But he hadn't been able to hide his feelings for Rachel. He couldn't take his eyes off her and sometimes he acted sillier than the sheep he looked after! Laban wasn't too surprised when Jacob asked his permission to marry Rachel. It was easy to persuade the boy to work for nothing for seven years in exchange for Rachel's hand in marriage, but there was a problem. If he let Rachel marry first, there would be no chance of Leah, his eldest daughter,

DO YOU LOVE SOMEONE ENOUGH TO WORK 14 YEARS WITHOUT PAY?

ever getting wed. There was no way Jacob would take Leah instead of Rachel, so a little deception was the only option. Laban was grateful that young women wore non-see-through veils on their wedding day!

The wedding day dawned and everything went well. There were crowds of people and Jacob and his bride had no time to themselves all day.

Early the next morning, as the daylight strengthened, Jacob turned to look tenderly at his new wife. Leah was lying beside him! Jacob nearly passed

## 5 THINGS JACOB DIDN'T KNOW ABOUT HIS WIFE

1. Her name
2. Her age
3. What she looked like
4. Who her sister was
5. Who she was

# COSTUMES FOR HIRE

GOATS' SKINS FOR THAT HAIRY MACHO FEELING

EXTRA HEAVY VEILS FOR THAT AIR OF MYSTERY

out from shock. His feelings ranged from anger and disappointment to humiliation. He discovered for himself that day what it felt like to be cheated, and it sickened him.

Laban stayed cool and calm in the face of Jacob's outrage. He pointed out that it was the custom for the eldest daughter to marry first, but that he was quite happy for Jacob to marry Rachel too—in exchange for another seven years free labor! Jacob knew when he was beaten. So he ended up with two wives, one who he loved to distraction and the other who he didn't care for at all. It was Leah though, who gave him six sons and the sisters' two slave-girls each bore Jacob two sons. Meanwhile Rachel almost gave up hope of becoming a mother. Finally she became pregnant and had a son, Joseph. She died giving birth to her second son, Benjamin. By the time he was born, Jacob had left Laban and had patched things up with Esau. He settled in Canaan, a rich man, the father of twelve sons, unaware that tragedy was about to strike.

# Family Favorites

Joseph's brothers hated him. But it really didn't bother Joseph. He put on the special coat Jacob had given him and set off for Shechem to check on them for his dad. The coat would remind them that he was the favorite son. As he walked along Joseph

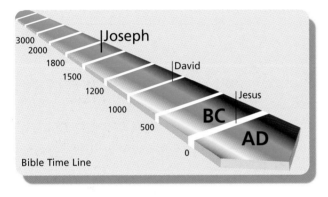

Bible Time Line

thought again about the dreams he'd had of everyone bowing down to him. He'd already described them to his family. It had caused a big upset, but he

was sure that one day his dreams would come true. What with his coat, his dreams and his habit of getting his brothers in trouble, just the mention of Joseph's name was enough to cause them to freak out.

Joseph didn't realize that his brothers had seen him approaching. By the time he reached them, they'd decided to sort him out once and for all. They forced him to the ground, ripped off his coat and dumped him, unceremoniously, down a dry well. Then they calmly ate their lunch and discussed how they were going to get away with murder. Bruised and shocked, Joseph huddled at the bottom of the well while his fate was being decided. Reuben, who was the eldest of the brothers, felt bad about the whole thing and suggested that they just leave him stuck down the

REUBEN

SIMEON

LEVI

JUDAH

DAN

NAPHTALI

GAD

You can read the full story in Genesis 37

home to show their father. Even though he was beside himself with grief, they let Jacob think that Joseph had been killed and eaten by a wild animal. Meanwhile, Joseph was alive and on his way to Egypt.

well. Secretly, he intended to come back later to rescue him.

Suddenly Joseph was hoisted out of the well. He looked on in amazement as his brother Judah haggled with a group of traders. Money changed hands and Joseph was dragged off behind one of the trader's camels. He'd been sold into slavery for twenty pieces of silver.

Thinking that was the last they'd ever see of him, Joseph's brothers tore his coat, smeared it with goat's blood and took it

JOSEPH WAS THE APPLE OF HIS FATHER'S EYE

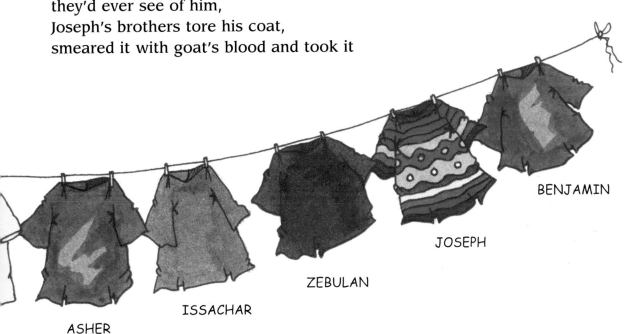

BENJAMIN

JOSEPH

ZEBULAN

ISSACHAR

ASHER

# From Rags to Riches

Joseph's brothers would never have recognized the spoiled brat they had sold into slavery. Joseph, who had never done a proper day's work in his life back at home, had been bought by Potiphar, an officer in the Egyptian army. Joseph had decided to make the best of the situation, and his hard work and honesty led Potiphar to put him in charge of his household and possessions. Unfortunately, he also came to the notice of Potiphar's wife. She was a bored, selfish woman who wanted Joseph to become her lover. When he refused, she exacted a terrible revenge.

She accused him of attempting to rape her. No one would listen to Joseph's version of events. He was thrown into jail for life.

Joseph moved quietly but confidently around the gloomy, dank dungeon. He had been a prisoner for years and his jailers always left his cell unlocked because he was so trustworthy and responsible. He stopped to talk sympathetically to two other prisoners, the king's baker and his wine steward. Both men were worried about the nightmares they had suffered.

Joseph explained that the baker's dream of birds eating the pastries from the baskets he was carrying on his head meant he was going to die. He told the wine steward, who had dreamed he was squeezing grape juice into the king's cup, that he was going to get his job back. Joseph asked him to mention his name to the king to help him get out of prison, but as soon as he was released, the wine steward forgot all about Joseph.

The king was really worried. Night after night his sleep was disturbed by weird dreams about thin cows eating up fat cows and thin ears of corn swallowing up full ones! Nobody could even begin to explain the dreams. Then the wine steward remembered Joseph.

Joseph had been waiting patiently for something to happen. At last men came for him. They gave him new clothes to

MUGSHOTS

SQUEEZE ME TIL THE PIPS SQUEAK

I KNEAD YOU

wear, then took him before the king. With God's help, he was able to interpret the king's dreams. He told him the dreams represented the years of good harvests that were to come and the years of famine. Joseph advised him to make preparations so that no one starved. The king was so impressed by Joseph that he put him in charge of the country, second only to him! Joseph, the spoiled son, the slave, the officer's servant, the lifer, was now the governor of Egypt, and it was nearly time for his brothers to appear on the scene again.

You can read the full story in Genesis 39–41

# A Change for the Better

Jacob couldn't bear the sound of his grandchildren crying for food. They were growing weaker every day. Then came news of corn in Egypt. There was no time to waste. Jacob sent his sons to Egypt straight away. Only Benjamin stayed with his father. Jacob had lost Joseph and there was no way he was going to let Joseph's younger brother out of his sight.

Joseph could hardly believe his eyes. There were his brothers bowing down before him. His dream had come true! They didn't recognize him and so he kept quiet. He decided to find out if they'd changed since they'd cold-heartedly sold him into slavery. Joseph treated them roughly, accused them of spying and sent them to jail. A few days later he released them so that they could fetch Benjamin to prove that they were telling the truth. Joseph kept Simeon as a hostage to make sure they came back.

WOW! I'VE HIT THE JACKPOT!

The brothers felt terrible, but their situation became even more scary when, on their way home, they discovered that the money they had paid for the corn was in the top of their sacks. What was happening to them and how were they going to explain it all to their father?

Jacob refused at first to let Benjamin go, but when the food ran out and they were faced with starvation again, he reluctantly agreed. They took gifts and the money they'd found in the sacks to Joseph. He welcomed them back and invited them to a meal. He still didn't reveal who he was but he made sure his younger brother, Benjamin, received five times as much to eat as the others!

Joseph's brothers had no idea that they had been set up. They left for home with sacks full of food only to be stopped and searched by Joseph's servants who insisted that one of the brothers had stolen a silver cup. During the search the cup was found in Benjamin's sack. Benjamin was condemned to slavery while the rest were free to continue their journey. Joseph couldn't wait for his brothers' reaction. Would they look out for themselves and abandon

## SPOT THE CUP!

JOSEPH'S LOST ONE OF HIS SILVER CUPS.
ANY IDEA WHERE IT'S HIDDEN?

## COMING AND GOING
### A CEREAL STORY

EPISODE 1 Joseph's brothers come to Egypt

EPISODE 2 They go home

EPISODE 3 They come back again

EPISODE 4 They go home again

EPISODE 5 They come back again

Benjamin to his fate, or had they changed?

Judah, who'd promised to bring Benjamin back safe and sound, fell to his knees. Tears ran down his face as he begged Joseph to punish him instead. He couldn't bear to see his little brother suffering or to bring more grief to his father. As he wept and pleaded, Joseph felt his own eyes filling with tears. He couldn't hide from them who he was any longer. When he saw how frightened they were, he had to reassure them that he was not out for revenge but wanted the whole family to join him in Egypt where they'd be safe from the famine. Jacob and the entire family moved to Egypt, little knowing that their descendants would still be there in four hundred years time—as slaves!

You can read the full story in Genesis 42–45

# A Basket Case

The baby's mother lived in constant fear. She was a Hebrew living in Egypt. She'd kept her son hidden for three months because she knew the Egyptians would kill him if they found him. Four hundred years had passed since Joseph had asked his father to bring the family to live in Egypt. During that time the number of their descendants had grown so much that they were seen as a threat to national security. Even though they had been made slaves, and were cruelly treated, the Hebrew population continued to increase. Finally, the king had ordered that all Egyptians should search out any newborn Hebrew boys and throw them into the River Nile.

The baby's mother was determined that her son would not die. In desperation, she hid him in a watertight basket among the reeds by the river's edge. She sent her daughter to keep watch a little distance from the hiding place.

THIS IS A VERY LONG BATH TIME!

Time passed. The mother found it impossible to concentrate on her housework. Then, suddenly, her daughter burst through the doorway, so excited she could hardly speak. She managed to tell her mother that the king's daughter, who came to bathe in the river every day, had found the baby! The princess wanted to keep him but she needed someone to feed and care for him until he was older so she'd offered to find a suitable person.

Abraham
|Moses
3000
2000
1500
1300
1200
1000
500
David
|Jesus
BC
AD
0

Bible Time Line

The baby was returned to his mother, who was paid by the princess to look after him! Later the princess adopted him, naming him Moses. The Hebrew baby had everything going for him as he grew up with all the privileges of a member of the Egyptian royal family.

Life should have been easy, but when Moses went out of the palace grounds and saw the suffering of his fellow Hebrews, he felt terrible. One day he saw an Egyptian beat a Hebrew slave to death. Moses couldn't control the rage that welled up inside him and he attacked and killed the man.

Certain that no one had seen him, he buried the body in the sand and returned to the palace. But Moses had been seen.

When he went back to the scene of the crime the next day he found two slaves fighting each other. When he tried to stop them, one of them asked him if he was going to kill him like he had the Egyptian.

Moses went cold. He realized that the news of what he'd done would already be spreading like wildfire. Being the princess' adopted son wouldn't save him. When the king heard what had happened, he declared that Moses would pay for it with his life. He had to catch him first though!

You can read the full story in Exodus 1, 2

# A Burning Issue

Moses made it across the border into Midian just in time. He'd left his old life behind him but he still acted impulsively. He didn't hesitate to act immediately when he saw a bunch of shepherds pushing some girls away from a well. He sorted the men out, then gave the girls' sheep and goats some water. They went straight home and told their father, Jethro, all about this gallant stranger from Egypt. Moses was invited to dinner and ended up working for Jethro and marrying Zipporah, one of his daughters.

Moses settled down to a peaceful, ordered life working as a shepherd and providing for his family. As he watched over the flocks out in the wilds of the desert near Sinai, thoughts of life in Egypt were far away. Then something happened that turned his life upside down.

Moses saw a bush that was on fire but amazingly it didn't disintegrate. He could hardly believe his eyes and moved closer to it. Then he heard God speaking directly to him, and he was more scared than when he had fled from Egypt. When he realized that God

WANTED FOR MURDER

wanted him to go back to Egypt and lead his people to freedom, Moses was horrified. It would mean laying his life on the line. He came up with several excuses but God countered each one and Moses finally accepted that he was going back.

With Jethro's agreement, Moses set out for Egypt with his wife and sons. His brother, Aaron, agreed to act as spokesman. They talked to the Hebrew leaders who were convinced that they had been sent by God. Feeling really encouraged, Moses and Aaron made arrangements to see the king.

They came straight to the point. The king's response was harsh and instant. He would not release the slaves. In fact he expected them to work harder. They'd always been supplied with straw for making bricks. In future they'd have to find their own straw and make the same number of bricks as before. They'd be far too busy to listen to people like Moses and Aaron ever again.

Moses and Aaron felt dreadful. The slaves were working until they dropped from exhaustion and those who failed to produce enough bricks were beaten. They felt very bitter towards Moses and Aaron who'd made life so much worse for them.

They had no other choice. Moses and Aaron had to go back to the king and ask again. They tried their best to persuade him, but the king wouldn't listen. It was going to take a long time and a lot of suffering before he gave in.

You can read the full story in Exodus 2–5

# A Safe Crossing

Moses struck the surface of the River Nile and the water ran red with blood. The king was stunned. It was the first of a series of plagues, but he refused to give in to Moses' demands to release his people. Even when gnats covered every living creature, when the animals died of a dreadful disease and when every Egyptian suffered from terrible boils, he still wouldn't listen. After the Egyptians' homes were filled with frogs, then with flies, when hailstorms destroyed the crops and trees and anyone in the open, when swarms of locusts ate every green thing and when there was total darkness for three days, he agreed to let the slaves go. Minutes later he changed his mind. But on the night that the first-born sons in every Egyptian family died, including his own son, the king finally gave in. He sent for Moses and Aaron and ordered them to take the people and get out of Egypt. They didn't hesitate. They'd waited too long for this moment.

But, as the shock died down, the king began to regret letting the slaves go. The country needed their free labor. He decided to bring them back by force.

The Israelites were trapped and terrified. The Red Sea stretched out in front of them and the Egyptian army was in hot pursuit. Moses had risked his life for his people but now they were turning on him. But Moses wasn't

AND NOW—THE WEATHER FORECAST!

scared any more. He knew he could trust God, and he wasn't disappointed. As the people continued to complain that they'd rather be slaves in Egypt than die in the desert, the wind began to pick up. It raged all night, blowing back the water. Led by Moses, the Israelites started to cross to the other side. They didn't go slowly. The Egyptians were gaining on them rapidly. They could hear the noise of their horses and chariots and the shouts of the soldiers. Some of the Israelites looked back to see how close they were. It was great! The Egyptians' chariots had sunk up to their axles in the wet seabed, and the men and horses couldn't move them. As they struggled, the last of the former slaves reached safety, the wind dropped and the water rushed back. Not one soldier in the Egyptian army survived.

The Israelites were free. Moses was their hero again. They thanked God for saving them from the Egyptians and their years of slavery, then the celebrations started in earnest but they didn't last long.

'AND THE OUTLOOK FOR TOMORROW, HEAVY SHOWERS OF FROGS ACROSS THE WHOLE COUNTRY ...'

You can read the full story in Exodus 7–14

# Count to Ten

Out in the desert, the Israelites completely blew it. It seemed ages since Moses had left them to climb Mount Sinai to be alone with God. He'd been gone so long they reckoned he'd never come back, so they made their own god to lead them out of that confronted him. They had all been through so much together, and though it had been hard, God had always been there for them. When they were thirsty, God provided them with fresh water; when they were hungry, he sent them manna and quails to eat; when they

the desert. They melted down their jewelry and made a statue of a golden calf. Then, after sacrificing to their idol, they let themselves go, celebrating and drinking too much. They didn't see Moses coming towards them carrying two stone tablets in his arms.

Moses could hardly take in the scene were attacked, God gave them the victory over their enemies. Yet, in no time at all, these people had forgotten what God had done for them. Engraved on the stone tablets Moses had brought down from the mountain were the laws God had given them to live by. If they obeyed the laws, they'd get their

# WARNING!

relationships with God and one another right. By the time Moses reached the foot of the mountain the people had already broken the first two commandments which said they must worship God alone and not make any idols. Disgusted and furious, Moses flung the stone tablets to the ground. They smashed into tiny pieces.

The Israelites soon sobered up when Moses made them melt down the calf. He had the gold ground into powder and mixed with water. Then he forced them to drink it. Everything had got completely out of control and they'd acted like idiots, but Moses was still prepared to meet with God on their behalf and ask his forgiveness. A second set of laws replaced the broken ones and they were carried in a special box as Moses and the people moved on towards the land God had promised them.

Moses never set foot in the Promised Land. He saw it from the top of Mount Pisgah but he died before they reached it. Joshua took over as Moses' successor. His task was to lead the Israelites into the Promised Land but thousands of people were already living there and they were prepared to die to keep the Israelites out.

You can read the full story in Exodus 16, 17, 20, 32; Deuteronomy 34

# Good Vibrations

The two men tried to lie perfectly still under the stalks of flax. If the soldiers found them they would kill them—after they'd tortured them. They could hear the soldiers questioning Rahab, the woman who was sheltering them. She agreed they'd entered her home but swore they'd left at sunset before the city gates were closed. The soldiers believed her. They sent orders to shut the city gates and the hunt continued.

As soon as the soldiers had gone, Rahab ran up to the roof where the men were hiding. She made them promise that when the Israelites attacked her city of Jericho, she and her family would be treated as kindly as she had treated them. They gave their word but told her that when the attack began she should hang a red cord from the window of her home, which was built into the city wall. Anyone in that marked house would be safe.

WILL YOU STOP **HANGING** AROUND!

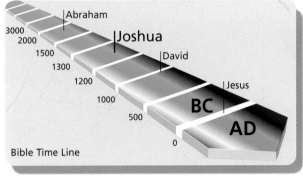

Bible Time Line

It was time for them to make their escape.

Under cover of darkness, Rahab lowered them down the wall on a rope. They took her advice and hid in the hills for three days before returning to their leader, Joshua.

Joshua had taken over when Moses

died. It had become his responsibility to lead the people across the River Jordan into the Promised Land. But first he needed to know the strength of the opposition they were going to face so he had chosen the two men to act as spies. When they returned they brought good news.

The people of Jericho had already heard all about the Israelites and were terrified of them! They had locked themselves inside the city gates for their own safety. No one could enter or leave. They could only watch in amazement as Joshua and his soldiers marched around the outside of the walled city day after day, blowing trumpets and stamping their feet. The soldiers were on their seventh circuit on the seventh day when the citizens heard a mighty shout after the trumpets had sounded. The city walls crumbled. Joshua's men clambered over the huge lumps of masonry and captured Jericho.

Everyone within the city died except for Rahab and her family. Rahab remembered what Joshua's men had told her to do. She believed they would keep the promise they'd made because she had saved their lives. She kept the door locked and barricaded, while

I KNOW YOU'RE IN CHARGE, JOSHUA, BUT I THINK WE'RE GOING AROUND IN CIRCLES!

outside it sounded as if the world was coming to an end. Then, at last, the two men she had hidden on her rooftop came to escort her and her relatives out of the house to a place of safety. Once they had left, Jericho was torched. It burned to the ground.

You can read the full story in Joshua 2, 6

31

# Pegged Out

Sisera was on the run. He was the commander of King Jabin of Hazor's army, one of the best equipped and most feared armies in the land, but he had just seen his forces wiped out in a battle against the Israelites. His men had barged around in total confusion and were slaughtered before his very eyes. Sisera had no intention of being a dead hero, so he leapt from his chariot and ran for his life. When he reached Jael's tent, Sisera thought he was safe. He knew Jael's husband and King Jabin were on good terms, so he didn't hesitate to ask her to hide him. He wasn't to know that he'd have stood a

I DON'T KNOW WHICH WAY TO TURN!

Abraham
3000
2000
1500
1300
1200
Deborah
David
1000
Jesus
500
BC
0
AD

Bible Time Line

better chance of survival if he'd stayed on the battlefield!

Barak, who'd been in charge of the victorious Israelite army, was in hot pursuit. He was determined to find Sisera and kill him. There were a lot of old scores to settle. The King of Hazor had made the Israelite people suffer for too long, subjecting them to sickening violence and cruelty. Deborah, one of the judges of Israel, had told Barak that God wanted him to get ten thousand men together and take on Sisera. With God's help, they defeated the enemy.

Jael welcomed Sisera into her tent and hid him behind a curtain. She gave him a drink of milk and promised to keep guard at the tent entrance and to turn away anyone who came looking for him. Sisera slipped into an exhausted sleep. Jael picked up a hammer and a wooden tent-peg and moved silently to where he lay. She knelt by his head, held the tent-peg against his skull, and hit it hard with the hammer.

Jael saw Barak approaching. She knew who he was looking for and took him into the tent. The commander hadn't stood a chance. Barak looked down at his dead body, then returned to his troops. They fought hard and finally destroyed their archenemy, the King of Hazor.

For many years, the Israelites lived in peace. But their peace was shattered when they became victims of Midianite raids. The Midianites killed, destroyed and devoured everything and everybody. The Israelites were forced to live in dens and caves like hunted animals. Once again they were in desperate need of help.

You can read the full story in Judges 4

33

# Who Me?

Gideon was on edge. He worked as quickly as he could but he kept looking over his shoulder. Like the rest of the Israelites, he lived in constant fear. The Midianites made their lives a misery. They stole their animals, attacked them when they tried to farm the land and destroyed any crops they succeeded in growing. Gideon knew that he wouldn't stand a chance if they saw him threshing the small amount of wheat he'd managed to harvest, but he risked it to keep his family alive.

EVERYONE WITH MUDDY KNEES—GO HOME!

Gideon was so busy working, and watching out for the Midianites, that he was totally unprepared for what happened next. God spoke directly to him and told him he must rescue his people. Gideon was shocked and horrified. Like Moses before him, he insisted that he was the wrong choice. Arguing was pointless. With God on his side he couldn't fail, but there was still a continuing doubt. Gideon decided to lay a fleece on the ground that night. If, the following morning, there was dew on the fleece but not on the ground around it, he'd be convinced that God was going to use him to rescue Israel. The next day Gideon wrung a bowlful of water out of the fleece and the ground was stone dry. But Gideon wanted to be extra sure, so he laid the fleece on the ground again. Would it be dry in the morning when the ground was wet? It was, and so Gideon knew he must fight, and defeat, the Midianites.

Thirty-two thousand Israelites volunteered to join Gideon to take on the Midianites, but first, Gideon had a couple of selection tests for them. He told them that anyone who was afraid should go home. Two thirds of his army left! Then he took the ten thousand volunteers who remained to the river and told them to drink. Most of them knelt down to drink. They were dismissed. Gideon kept the three hundred men who had scooped up the water in their hands. They had proved they were alert and ready for action.

GIDEON'S VERSION OF SON ET LUMIÈRE

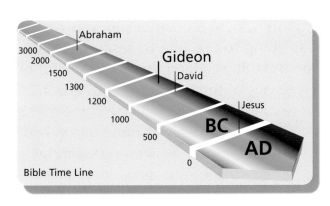

It seemed impossible that three hundred men could defeat the Midianite hordes, but that night Gideon and his servant crept into the Midianite camp. They overheard two soldiers saying they were convinced that Gideon and his men were going to win. Gideon felt confidence flood through him.

It was not quite midnight. The Midianites awoke with a start. Trumpets were blaring, men were shouting and blazing torches dazzled their eyes. They grabbed their swords and attacked the shadowy figures who swarmed around them. They ran and tried to fight their way to safety but they were so frightened and confused they didn't realize they were killing their own men. Gideon and his gallant three hundred wiped out the Midianite army, armed only with trumpets and torches. They didn't strike a single blow! It was a great victory, but the Israelites weren't going to enjoy peace for very long.

You can read the full story in Judges 6, 7

# Trials of Strength

Samson was the strongest, most fearless man alive. His reputation grew as news spread of how he had killed a lion with his bare hands

I'M SORRY, SAMSON'S TIED UP AT THE MOMENT!

and slaughtered one thousand of the Israelites' enemies, the Philistines, armed only with a dead donkey's jawbone. They were desperate to capture him, but first they needed to discover the secret of his phenomenal strength. Samson wasn't telling, but he did have one weakness they could exploit. He couldn't cope with being nagged.

Delilah, Samson's Philistine wife,

never shut up. The Philistine kings had offered to give her over five thousand pieces of silver if she found out what made her husband so strong. She kept on and on at Samson. At first he tried to humor her. He told her that if she tied him up with seven new bowstrings he'd be as weak as anybody else. He let her do it, but when she shouted 'The Philistines are coming!' he snapped the bowstrings like threads. Delilah was not amused. He'd lied to her. She kept up the nagging and Samson kept stringing her along. He made out that being tied with new ropes would do the trick, but as soon as she shouted a warning, he broke the ropes easily. Then he pretended that having the locks of his hair woven into a loom would render him powerless, but once again, at the

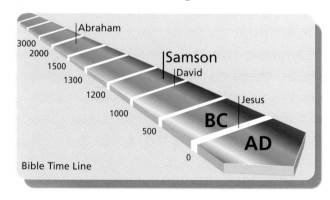

Bible Time Line

3000
2000
1500
1300
1200
1000
500
0
Abraham
Samson
David
Jesus
BC
AD

36

crucial moment, he pulled his hair loose. Delilah flew into a rage. She complained that he didn't love her and wouldn't let the subject drop. At last, exhausted and fed up, Samson told her the truth. He would lose his strength if his hair was cut.

HE SHOULD BE PUT IN A DEADLOCK, NOT DREADLOCKS!

Delilah sent for her money. When Samson was fast asleep she signaled to the man who had brought her the cash to cut off Samson's hair. Then Delilah woke him. The Philistines took him easily. His strength had gone. They blinded him and put him in prison.

A great roar went up as the small boy led Samson into the temple. It was a festival day and the Philistines wanted to see Samson standing helpless before them. He was blind and in chains and the Philistines jeered and mocked him. The boy left him standing between two great pillars in full view of his tormentors.

Samson stretched out his hands and rested them on the stone pillars. He could see nothing, but he could hear the Philistines' taunts. Once they'd have run for their lives at the mention of his name. Now they laughed at him, because they thought he was weak and helpless. But since his capture his hair had grown again. Samson prayed to God to give him back his strength just once more. Then he pushed against the pillars with all his might. They cracked and gave way. The temple roof collapsed and everyone, including Samson, died in the ruins.

You can read the full story in Judges 14–16

37

# A Happy Ending

Naomi made a momentous decision. She was old and on her own in a foreign country. Her sons and husband were dead. She was going to walk back to Judah, her homeland. It would be a long, dangerous journey, but she wanted to be with her own people, not in Moab.

Naomi, Elimelech and their sons had only moved to Moab as a temporary measure because of the famine in Judah. They'd stayed on longer than they'd planned, and the boys had grown up and married local girls. Then tragedy struck. First Elimelech died and later both their sons. Now, at the beginning of the long trek back to Judah, Naomi told her daughters-in-law, Orpah and Ruth, that they must go home. They were in tears and swore they wouldn't leave her, but Naomi insisted. Their parents would almost certainly find them Moabite

husbands, then they'd be settled and happy again.

Ruth stood next to Naomi and watched Orpah turn for home. She

refused to listen to Naomi as she pleaded with her to go with Orpah. There was no way she would let this elderly woman face the future alone. Ruth put her arms around Naomi and promised she'd never leave her. She was so determined that Naomi gave in and they set off for Bethlehem.

The two women reached their destination unscathed, but their troubles were not over. Somehow they had to find enough food to keep

Abraham
3000
2000
1500
1300
1200
1000
500
Ruth
David
Jesus
BC
AD
0
Bible Time Line

themselves alive. The barley was being harvested and Ruth suggested that she went to the fields to pick up any grains the farm workers had missed. Naomi agreed and before long Ruth was working in the fields of a rich landowner called Boaz.

Boaz decided to check up on how the harvest was progressing. As he talked to his foreman, he noticed Ruth hard at work. He asked about her, and what he heard impressed him. He discreetly ordered the reapers to drop large amounts of grain for Ruth to pick up.

HE SAYS, 'LEAVE PLENTY OF GRAIN BEHIND.' I SAY 'WHAT HAPPENS TO OUR PRODUCTIVITY BONUS!'

Naomi was delighted to discover that Ruth had been working in Boaz's fields. Boaz was a relation, and he'd clearly taken to her daughter-in-law! Once the harvest was over, Naomi planned some positive matchmaking. She told Ruth to dress up, put on plenty of perfume and spend the night at the threshing place where Boaz would be. No one must know she was there, but she should make sure she was near Boaz after he'd gone to sleep.

Boaz was shocked when he woke up during the night and found Ruth lying at his feet. She calmly asked him to marry her! He promised to take care of her and Naomi but told Ruth to leave before the others awoke.

Everyone approved of the marriage. In time, Ruth gave birth to a son whom they named Obed. Naomi moved in with them and looked after the baby. She'd faced starvation, bereavement and poverty but at last her life had a happy ending.

You can read the full story in Ruth 1–4

# Dedicated Service

Samuel woke up suddenly. Someone was calling his name. He ran barefoot to Eli's bedroom, but the old priest denied calling him

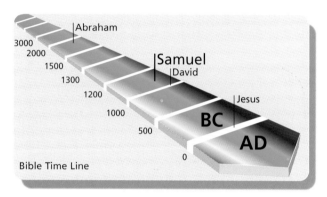

Bible Time Line

3000
2000
1500
1300
1200
1000
500
0
Abraham
Samuel
David
Jesus
BC
AD

and sent him back to bed. Samuel had just settled down when again he heard someone call his name. For the second time he ran to see what Eli wanted. Again he was told to go to bed. Eli had not called him. When it happened the third time, Samuel got out of bed and wondered what Eli would say this time.

Eli lay awake thinking about Samuel. He wouldn't be lying. Eli knew him too well. After all, he'd brought him up from a toddler when the boy's mother, Hannah, had handed him over.

Eli remembered the first time he'd seen Hannah on the steps of the temple. Hannah was praying but she was in such a state that he thought she was drunk! Only she wasn't drunk, just distraught with misery and hopelessness. Her husband, Elkanah, was a good man, but his other wife, Peninnah, tormented and humiliated Hannah because, unlike her, Hannah had no children. Hannah had pleaded with God for a child and promised that if her prayers were answered she would dedicate him to His service as soon as he was old enough to leave her. God had answered Hannah's prayers. Samuel had come to live at the temple.

Hannah brought him a new tunic as a birthday

HAPPY BIRTHDAY SAMUEL!

OH, GREAT A NEW COAT, I'D NEVER HAVE GUESSED

present every year.

It was clear to Eli that the boy was being called by God, so when Samuel came into his bedroom the third time, Eli explained it was God who was calling him and told Samuel to go back to bed. If he heard the voice again he was to say he was listening. When his name was called, Samuel followed Eli's instructions. God spoke to him and gave him some grim news about Eli's family.

When morning came, Samuel got up and reluctantly went to open the temple doors. He was afraid of meeting Eli. How could he tell this kind man that tragedy lay ahead for him and his family?

Eli sat by the roadside staring into space. Many years had passed since he'd asked Samuel to tell him what God had said to him that night in his room. What he heard had been bad enough, but now the situation was far worse. After the Philistines had defeated them in battle, the Israelites had carried the Ark of the Covenant, the symbol of God's presence, around with them. It gave them confidence, but Eli was sick with worry over its safety. When he saw a man running down the road towards Shiloh he feared the worst. The messenger brought terrible news. They'd fought the Philistines again and they'd lost. Their enemies had seized the Ark of the Covenant and Eli's sons were among the dead. Eli fell backwards with shock. As he hit the ground he broke his neck and died instantly.

You can read the full story in 1 Samuel 1–4

# Slung Out

Samuel was embarrassed and scared. He'd traveled to Bethlehem to see a man called Jesse, convinced that God wanted him to anoint one of Jesse's sons as king. If Saul, the ruling king, ever found out what he was doing, he'd kill him. Saul

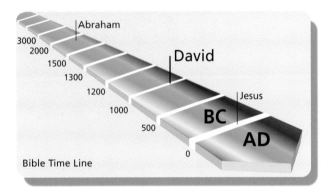

was the first ever Israelite king. Samuel had advised the Israelites against having a king, but they'd insisted. Saul had failed to live up to expectations. Now Samuel had to find the right person to succeed him.

Seven of Jesse's sons paraded in front of Samuel. They were all tall and good looking but not one of them was God's choice of king. Samuel had to reject each of them. Feeling quite desperate, he asked Jesse if he had any other sons. Jesse sent for his youngest son, David.

From the first minute he saw David, Samuel knew that he was meant to be king.

David was stunned when Samuel anointed him in front of his elder brothers. He was the baby of the family, and he'd never considered himself to be anyone special. Even now he was going to have to wait many years before he became king but from that moment his life changed forever. He received an invitation to the royal court to play to the king. Saul was suffering from bouts of deep depression. David's harp playing soothed him.

Saul soon had to deal with a critical situation. The old enemy, the Philistines, were camped, ready to do battle with the Israelite army. Every day they sent Goliath, a giant of a man, to challenge them to a man-to-man contest. The winner's side would be given the victory but not one Israelite was prepared to take up the challenge.

One day Jesse asked David to take some food to his three eldest brothers who were in the army. David heard Goliath's challenge and saw the terror on the Israelites' faces. He was horrified that no one would fight Goliath and

## NEWS FLASH    GOLIATH LOSES HIS HEAD!

decided he would take him on. Saul was against it. The idea was ludicrous. David was only a boy while Goliath was a soldier several times his size. David refused to be put off. As a shepherd he'd fought off bears and lions and, in any case, God was with him so he couldn't fail. Armed only with his shepherd's crook and a sling, David walked towards Goliath. On the way, he picked up five smooth stones from the stream.

Goliath couldn't believe his eyes. This had to be a joke, or was it the worst possible kind of insult? He threatened David but David was no more scared by his words than he was by Goliath's size and reputation. As Goliath moved towards him, David placed a stone in his sling, took aim and slung it. The stone hit Goliath on the forehead. He crashed to the ground. David cut off Goliath's head with his sword. The Philistines fled, pursued by the Israelites who had suddenly regained their courage.

David became a hero overnight, mobbed by adoring crowds wherever he went, but his popularity led to jealousy, and jealousy led to attempts on his life.

You can read the full story in 1 Samuel 16, 17

# Firm Friends

The spear thudded into the wall missing David's head by a hair's breadth. David, who had ducked instinctively, looked up for a moment, horrified and shocked at what had happened. Another spear whistled past his head as he threw himself to one side.

Saul wished the spear had killed David. He hated him for his victory over Goliath which had made him the people's hero, for being successful in every mission he tackled and for his popularity with his fellow soldiers. He decided to send him to fight the Philistines in the hope that he'd die leading them into

battle. But David didn't die; he won and his popularity grew.

Next, the king tried a more subtle approach to rid himself of this man who had everything that he lacked. He said David could marry his daughter, Merab, if he served him bravely by fighting his enemies. Saul was convinced that David would be killed if he were involved in enough battles. David, though, continued to prove a successful leader, returning from war without so much as a scratch. When the time came, Saul gave Merab to another man. It didn't matter to David because Saul's other daughter, Michal, was in love with him and wanted to marry him. Saul saw another opportunity to use the Philistines to kill David. He agreed to

I DIDN'T THINK MY PLAYING WAS THAT BAD!

44

the marriage as long as David killed one hundred Philistines. David killed two hundred Philistines and married Michal.

Michal knew her father was determined to kill David but he wasn't going to succeed if she had anything to do with it. She made up the bed to look as though someone was asleep in it. It wouldn't fool the guards for long but it might give David a little more precious time in which to get clear of his home. The men watching the house hadn't seen her lower David out of the window. It wasn't long before they were hammering on her door. They wanted David, but Michal convinced them that he was ill and so they reported back to Saul. Saul was quite happy to kill him in his bed and sent the guards back to get David. They soon discovered they'd been tricked. Saul was so furious with Michal that she had to pretend that David had threatened to kill her if she didn't help him. Meanwhile David stayed with Samuel.

Jonathan, Saul's son, was sick of the way his father was behaving. He and David were close friends, and when David asked him to find out why Saul

YOU'LL NEVER WAKE HIM!!

wanted to kill him, Jonathan promised to do what he could. They decided on a signal which would tell David whether his life was still in danger or if it was safe for him to return to court. Jonathan had spoken up for David before, but this time as soon as he mentioned David's name, Saul flew into a rage. He flung a spear at Jonathan, screaming that he was a traitor. Jonathan realized that his father was determined to kill his friend. The next morning he went to the field where David was hiding and gave the danger signal. From now on, David was forced to be an outlaw, constantly on the run.

You can read the full story in 1 Samuel 18–20

# Undercover

David shrank back against the walls of the cave. Saul was standing just inside the entrance. David knew the king was determined to kill him but until now he had managed to keep a step ahead of Saul and his three thousand first-rate troops. Someone had betrayed him and told Saul where he was hiding. David signaled to his men to keep quiet, but they whispered urgently to him to kill Saul while he was on his own. David crept up behind him, a knife in his hand. With extreme care, he cut off a piece of Saul's cloak, then slipped back into the depths of the cave. Saul didn't feel a thing. Once he'd left the cave, David followed at a distance, then shouted to get his attention. David held up the piece of cloth as proof that he was a loyal subject who would never hurt his king. Saul felt sick at heart. Tears ran down his cheeks as he humbly admitted that he was in the wrong. Saul went home, but David realized that he would probably turn on him again, so he moved to another area.

David and his men lived peaceably, treating the inhabitants well. One of them, however, made the mistake of crossing David. Nabal was a rich man and was married to a beautiful, intelligent woman, Abigail, but he was mean and bad tempered. When some of David's men asked him to provide some food, Nabal refused point-blank. It was a foolish thing to do. David felt deeply insulted and decided to sort him out. He set out with four hundred armed men but found Abigail blocking his way. She threw herself at his feet and he accepted the bread, meat, fruit

IT'S SUCH A RELIEF TO BE ON MY OWN!

and wine she had brought. Although she begged him to ignore Nabal's behavior, David still wanted to confront him. Abigail refused to give in. Finally, she convinced David not to take revenge but to leave it to God to punish his enemies.

David turned back, pleased that he had made the right decision and most impressed with Abigail. He had no idea then that, within a short time, she would become his wife. Abigail reached home to find Nabal dead drunk. The next morning she told him all that had happened. Nabal collapsed and died a few days later.

As soon as he heard the news, David proposed to Abigail. She accepted without hesitation. Saul was overwhelmed with jealousy again. He set out to kill David but David's spies told him where Saul had camped. Everyone was asleep when David and two of his men entered the camp at night. They stood next to Saul whose spear lay alongside him. One of David's men wanted to use it to kill Saul but David stopped him. Instead, they walked out of the camp taking with them Saul's spear and

water jar. When they were safely across the valley, David shouted to Saul and held up the proof of how close to death he had been. As before, he vowed he would never harm his king. Once again

I THINK THE KING NEEDS TO TIGHTEN UP ON SECURITY!

Saul said he'd been a fool and asked David to return to court, but David couldn't trust him. He thought he'd be safer with his enemies, so he left to live among the Philistines!

You can read the full story in 1 Samuel 24–26

# Affairs of the Heart

David was king at last. Saul and Jonathan had been killed fighting the Philistines and so he became ruler, first of Judah, and then Israel too. He was popular with the people and successful on the battlefield, but life had some cruel surprises for him.

Although he was already married,

LOVE AT FIRST SIGHT

David had fallen in love with Bathsheba. She was beautiful, but she was married to Uriah, an officer in David's army. When she told David she was expecting his baby, he had to do something quickly. David was cold and calculating. He arranged for Uriah to be killed. David's army was fighting the Ammonites so he ordered Joab, his army commander, to put Uriah in the front line where the fighting was heaviest, then to retreat, leaving him to be killed. Joab obeyed. Soon afterwards David received a report from Joab listing the officers who had been killed. Uriah was among the dead.

Bathsheba married David once the time of mourning was over. She gave birth to a son whom David adored, but, within weeks, the baby fell ill and died. David blamed himself. One day, Samuel's successor, Nathan, visited David. He told him about a rich man who had many cattle and sheep, and a poor man who only had one lamb which he loved like a daughter. A visitor arrived at the rich man's house needing to be fed. Rather than kill one of his own animals, the rich man took and killed the poor man's lamb. David believed Nathan was describing a genuine incident. He was so indignant that he declared that the heartless rich man should die. Then Nathan pointed out that he had condemned himself. David was the rich man in the story. He was the king. He had everything but still he took another man's wife. David was devastated at what he had done and was truly sorry that he'd abused his power and position.

Life had to go on. David had to get over the death of his baby son and deal with the country's enemies. The worst crisis of all was the one created by his eldest son, Absalom. Absalom was violent, deceitful and obsessed with power. He turned some people against his father, then raised an army and challenged David to battle.

David could never think of Absalom as his enemy, but he had to deal with the rebellion. He ordered that Absalom should not be harmed, then waited anxiously for news. It came at last. After a long and furious battle, David's army won. But David was only interested in Absalom's safety. A slave told him that Absalom had escaped from the battlefield. As he rode through a forest his long hair got caught up in the branches of a tree and he was left hanging there, helpless. Joab came upon him and drove three spears through his body, then buried him in a pit in the forest. David wept. Victory had brought only grief and

A HAIR-RAISING ENDING

heartache. But there was still some joy in his life. He and Bathsheba did have another son who grew up to be almost as famous as his father. His name was Solomon.

You can read the full story in 2 Samuel 11, 12, 18

49

# Food Aid

Solomon had made a name for himself. He'd built the stupendous Temple and a fabulous palace, and gained a reputation for wisdom. But when his son became king, the tribes rebelled and the kingdom split into two, Israel in the north and Judah in the south.

Over the years which followed, Israel became a nation of idol worshipers. One king, Ahab, even built a temple to a god called Baal. He and his wife Jezebel regarded anyone who remained true to God, like Elijah, as their enemies.

The people of Israel were dropping like flies. The earth was dry and cracked. No rain fell and no crops grew. Elijah had survived the drought and famine so far because he'd camped by a brook and ravens had brought him food. Then the brook dried up and he had to move on. He approached the town gates of Zarephath. There was no sign of life apart from a woman slowly and painfully gathering firewood.

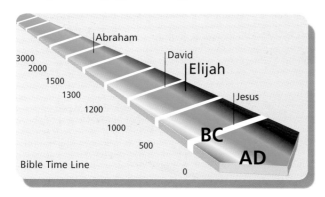

The widow was resigned to death. She only had a handful of flour and a drop of olive oil left. Once she'd collected enough wood she'd light a fire and cook one last meal for herself and her son. Then they'd starve to death like so many others. She didn't notice the stranger until he spoke. To her amazement he asked to share her final meal. She wasn't sure why she agreed. He'd promised that her flour and oil would not run out until the rains came, but she found that difficult to believe. Still she couldn't refuse him, and sure enough the flour and oil didn't run out, but something more shocking happened.

The widow's son fell ill. Just as she'd started to hope that they would survive the drought and famine he got worse and worse and then he died. The woman was beside herself with grief. A child shouldn't die before his parents. She turned on Elijah. There was no one else to blame and she wanted to vent her anger on someone. It must be his fault. He'd walked into their lives uninvited. They'd shared all they had with him and this was the result.

Elijah took the boy from her. He laid him on the bed, stretched himself out on him and prayed from the bottom of his heart. His prayers were answered. The boy began to breathe unaided and regained consciousness. Elijah carried

him downstairs to his mother. The widow knew for certain now that Elijah was no ordinary man, but a man of God.

The drought was into its third year. King Ahab was a worried man. As he searched for some sign of grass that would keep his horses alive, Elijah confronted him. Bravely Elijah told Ahab the truth. Although he was the king, he'd disobeyed God's commands.

He worshiped idols of the false god, Baal. Ahab glared at Elijah but when Elijah issued a challenge to him and the prophets of Baal, he just couldn't ignore it.

You can read the full story in 1 Kings 17

# The Big Match

**B**lood poured from cuts all over their bodies yet they still inflicted more wounds on themselves. They were moving around more slowly now and their voices were hoarse after hours of ranting and raving, begging their god, Baal, to light the fire under their sacrificial bull. Elijah watched in silence. Earlier he'd made fun of them, suggesting that Baal might have gone away or was day-dreaming or asleep. The prophets of Baal responded by praying louder and dancing harder. Then they

WHY DIDN'T SOMEONE BRING SOME MATCHES?

began to cut themselves with knives, but still nothing happened.

Elijah had arranged to meet King Ahab and the prophets of Baal on Mount Carmel. The king had summoned the Israelite people to watch as Elijah challenged the prophets of Baal to demonstrate the power of their god. It was a simple challenge. They had to kill a bull, cut it up and place it on a pile of wood. Elijah would do the same with his bull. Then the prophets of Baal had to pray to their god to light the fire and Elijah would pray to his God. The one who answered the prayers would be seen to be the true God and the Israelites would know who to worship. Elijah gave the opposition their turn first. They pleaded with their god for hours but nothing happened.

Now it was Elijah's turn. The people watched as he took twelve stones and built an altar. He dug a trench around it, placed the wood on the altar, cut up the bull and laid it on the wood. They gasped as he poured so much water over the sacrifice that it became sodden and the trench overflowed. Silence fell as Elijah prayed simply and quietly. Suddenly, the wood burst into a great blaze and the flames incinerated the bull, the wood and even the stones. The earth was scorched and the water in the trench boiled and evaporated in the great heat. The Israelites flung themselves to the ground and declared Elijah's God was the true God. The prophets of Baal stood open-mouthed in amazement. Before they could get away, the people seized them, dragged them down the mountainside and killed them.

WE WANT A BURNT SACRIFICE NOT A DROWNED ONE!

King Ahab returned to the palace. As he described to Queen Jezebel what had happened on Mount Carmel, she grew mad with anger. She threatened to kill Elijah for what he'd done to her prophets. Elijah knew this was no empty threat. He went into hiding and lived in terror of Jezebel. One day, as he stood on Mount Sinai, he thought about his situation and felt totally miserable. He'd always served God, but his people, the Israelites, had turned to idol worship and had killed God's prophets. Now there was only him left and they wanted to kill him too. As he stood there, alone, a hurricane force wind came from nowhere, splitting rocks in two and opening up the hillside. Elijah had scarcely recovered from the shock when an earthquake shook the ground beneath his feet and fires broke out across the mountainside. When it subsided Elijah heard the soft whisper of a voice telling him to come out of hiding and go back to where the action was. He had some vital work to do, including sorting out Ahab and Jezebel.

You can read the full story in 1 Kings 18, 19

# A Miscarriage of Justice

Jezebel couldn't understand her husband. Ahab was such a wimp. If things didn't go his way, he sulked. He was the king and yet he had no idea how to use his power. She went into his room. He was lying on his bed facing the wall and refusing to eat. Jezebel sat beside him and persuaded him to tell her why he was so depressed. It was all over a vineyard which was near the palace. He'd asked the owner, Naboth, to sell it to him or exchange it for another piece of land. Naboth had refused because the vineyard had always been in his family and he wanted to hand it down to his sons. Ahab had gone away disappointed and frustrated. He'd really wanted the vineyard but he'd failed to get it. Jezebel couldn't believe how easily he'd given in, but she just made encouraging noises. She told Ahab to cheer up and leave everything to her. She'd get the vineyard for him.

Jezebel was a clever and unscrupulous woman. She planned to engineer Naboth's death in such a way that Ahab, as king, could confiscate his vineyard. As Naboth was a law-abiding, God-fearing man, she needed all her skill to plot his downfall. Jezebel sat down and wrote to some city officials and leading citizens. She forged Ahab's name and used his royal seal. The letters told them to arrange a festival at which Naboth should be given the place of honor. During the celebrations two men must come forward and accuse Naboth of cursing God and the king. The penalty for such a crime was execution. The men did as they were ordered, then they took Naboth out of the city and stoned him to death. When Jezebel received the message that Naboth was dead, she went to her husband

I THOUGHT THESE MIGHT MAKE YOU FEEL BETTER!

IT'S VINE, ALL VINE!!

and told him he could take possession of the vineyard.

Ahab didn't hesitate, nor did he ask a single question. He just took what he wanted, but he and Jezebel couldn't escape the consequences of their actions.

Just as Ahab was enjoying his new acquisition, he was confronted by a very stern-looking Elijah. Ahab had always regarded him as his enemy, but what Elijah said had a devastating effect on him. Elijah reminded him of all the wrong things he had done and warned that disaster awaited him and his family, including Jezebel. Ahab tore his clothes and wore sackcloth smeared with ashes. He refused food and went around looking gloomy and feeling desperately depressed.

Disaster struck some years on. Ahab died in battle. He'd disguised himself, hoping to cheat death, but an arrow pierced his armor and he bled to death. Jezebel met her end later. She was thrown from a palace window, and the new king of Israel, Jehu, drove his chariot over her body.

You can read the full story in 1 Kings 21

# Obeying Instructions

Naaman looked with distaste at the River Jordan flowing past him just a yard or two away. He was still feeling angry and humiliated. He'd come all the way from Syria to see Elijah's successor, Elisha. He'd been told Elisha could cure his dreadful skin disease but Elisha had just sent a servant to tell him to go and bathe in the river seven times. He'd stormed off, outraged. Elisha hadn't even come out of his house to meet

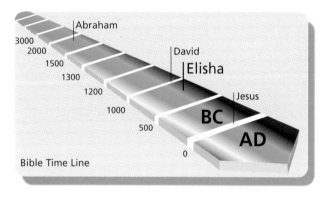

Bible Time Line

him and anyway, if he had to go bathing, the rivers in Syria were far superior to the Jordan. He might as well forget the whole idea, go back home and get on with his job as commander of the Syrian army.

He'd been silly to listen to the young Israelite girl he'd captured during a raid. Now his wife's maidservant, she had told her mistress that Elisha would cure Naaman. He'd set out, full of optimism, with plenty of silver, gold and fine clothes as gifts. When he finally

found Elisha this was the result—a huge let-down.

Naaman's servant knew his master well. He calmed him down and persuaded him to follow Elisha's instructions. After immersing himself in the water seven times, Naaman climbed up the bank on to dry land. All signs of his disease had gone. His skin was firm and clear. He was cured and he couldn't wait to praise God, thank Elisha and give him one of the gifts he'd brought from Syria. Elisha, though, refused, much to the amazement of his servant, Gehazi. If Elisha didn't want what Naaman was offering, Gehazi certainly did, but Naaman had already set off for home.

Gehazi found it impossible to stand by and let Naaman take the silver, gold and finery back to Syria when they could be his for the asking. He ran after

You can read the full story in 2 Kings 5

Naaman and told him that Elisha had changed his mind—he had guests and wanted to give them some presents. Naaman gladly handed over six thousand pieces of silver and two sets of fine clothes. Gehazi carried them back and hid them in Elisha's house. When Elisha asked where he had been, Gehazi lied to get himself out of trouble, but it was no use. Elisha knew what he had been up to and dismissed him with a warning about what was going to happen to him. By the time Gehazi had packed and was ready to leave, his skin was badly affected by the same disease from which Naaman had just been cured.

# Murder Most Foul

**X**erxes, the Emperor of Persia and ruler of one hundred and twenty-seven provinces stretching from India to Sudan, loved partying. He was certainly enjoying the huge banquet at his winter residence. It had already lasted for a week and his guests were impressed by the lavish hospitality. By day seven the amount they'd been drinking was having an effect. Xerxes, having drunk too much himself, decided to show off his queen, Vashti. He ordered her to appear dressed in her royal regalia. To his horror, Vashti defiantly refused to come. Xerxes was furious. She'd made him look a fool and

choose a new queen from a selection of the most beautiful young girls to be found in his empire.

Esther didn't know what lay ahead when she was escorted to the palace. An orphan, she lived

```
Bible Time Line
3000
  2000        Abraham
    1500
      1300              David
        1200                 |Esther
          1000                  |Jesus
            500          BC
                    0          AD
```

her behavior might influence other women to have no respect for their husbands. Xerxes had to restore his authority. He stripped Vashti of her position as queen, but it wasn't enough. He still couldn't forget her and what she'd done to him. Then his advisers came up with a brilliant idea. He should

QUEEN VASHTI REFUSES TO MAKE A GUEST APPEARANCE

with her cousin Mordecai. When her parents died Mordecai adopted her and treated her like a daughter. Every day she was at the palace he managed to speak to her and she took his advice, keeping the fact that she was Jewish a secret. Along with the other girls, she was put on a special diet and given regular beauty treatments for a whole year. Then each one of them was sent for, in turn, by Xerxes.

Xerxes looked at the girl standing before him. She was only one of countless young women who had paraded in front of him recently, but Esther was different. Xerxes liked her more than any of the others. He decided that she should be the new queen and arranged a great banquet in Esther's honor. He even gave Mordecai an administrative position in the royal household. It was an appointment that would save his life. During his time as one of Xerxes' officials, Mordecai uncovered a plot to assassinate the king. Following an investigation, the traitors were hanged.

For Esther, life was good. The king loved her and her cousin was never far away. Then everything went horribly wrong. Xerxes appointed one of his noblemen, Haman, as prime minister. He ordered every official to show their respect to Haman by kneeling down before him. Mordecai refused. He disapproved of Haman's appointment. He would not bow down to a man who was totally unscrupulous. Mordecai knew he was asking for trouble but he wouldn't give in. He even told the other officials that he was a Jew and they told Haman all about him. A resentful and vindictive man, Haman enjoyed plotting his bloodthirsty revenge. Not only would he have Mordecai put to death, but he would order the massacre of every Jew in the Persian Empire.

You can read the full story in Esther 1–3

# Just Desserts

Esther was deeply disturbed. She'd heard that Mordecai was in mourning but she didn't know why. No one had told her Haman had convinced the king that there were dangerous people in the empire who should be exterminated or that Xerxes had given Haman the authority to get rid of them. Then Mordecai sent her a copy of Haman's proclamation. It specified the day on which all the Jews in the empire were to be slaughtered and their possessions confiscated.

Mordecai begged her to go to the king and plead for the lives of her people.

Esther, dressed in her royal robes, waited outside the throne room. She was scared but determined. She knew she was breaking the law by going to see the king when he hadn't summoned her. The penalty was death unless the king held out his golden scepter to her. Then her life would be spared. Esther, and all the Jews in the city, had been fasting and praying for three days and nights in preparation for this moment. When Xerxes held out his scepter towards her and asked what she wanted, Esther was so relieved she could scarcely speak. She took a deep breath and invited Xerxes and Haman to dinner that night.

The dinner party was a great success. Xerxes was intrigued. He was sure Esther wanted something but, when he asked her during the meal, she just invited him and Haman to dine with her again the next night.

Back in his room, Xerxes couldn't sleep. He started reading the official records and came across the account of how Mordecai had saved his life. He was upset when he discovered that Mordecai had never been rewarded for what

AND WE ALL THOUGHT HAMAN HATED MORDECAI!

he'd done and decided to make amends.

Throughout the night carpenters worked at building a gallows on Haman's orders. Haman wanted to see Mordecai hanging from them before he joined the king and queen for dinner again. All he needed was the king's permission but, before he could ask, Xerxes sent for him for advice about honoring a man he wanted to reward. Haman felt good. The king was obviously talking about him! Haman suggested dressing the man in royal robes and leading him through the city on horseback so everyone could see how much the king favored him. Xerxes agreed with him and sent for robes and a horse for Mordecai. Haman was stunned, but worse was to follow. He had to dress his enemy in the robes and

lead him through the city. Haman felt totally humiliated, but he still had to attend Esther's dinner.

Xerxes didn't understand. When he asked Esther what she wanted, she begged him to let her and her people live. He had to admit that he didn't know that there was a decree condemning all the Jews to death. Esther told him that Haman was the man who had ordered their slaughter. Haman stared at them both in terror. When the king stormed out into the garden, Haman threw himself down before Esther, pleading for mercy, but before the night was out he was hanged on the gallows built for Mordecai.

You can read the full story in Esther 4–7

# Listen and Learn

Jeremiah sank deeper into the mud at the bottom of the well. He looked up at the patch of sky far above his head. He knew now that he'd been left to starve to death. His enemies, the leading men in Judah, had finally succeeded in stopping him from telling his fellow countrymen the truth.

He begged them to turn back to God but nobody had wanted to listen. Once he'd lifted a large clay pot above his head and hurled it to the ground in front of the elders and priests. It smashed to smithereens. He told them that this was how God would destroy the people of Judah if they continued to worship Baal and other false gods, but they ignored him. He persisted, though, even when things turned nasty. There was the time he stood in the Temple courtyard and prophesied disaster at the top of his voice until the guards marched him away. They beat

JEREMIAH'S SMASHING MESSAGE

him up and left him in chains near the Temple Gate, but that didn't stop him. As soon as he was released, he went to the Temple again, only to be seized, threatened and then banned.

Then there was the scroll. He dictated to his friend, Baruch, everything God had told him. If the people realized what was going to happen to them, they might turn from their evil ways. He desperately wanted them to listen and repent. When the scroll was complete, he asked Baruch

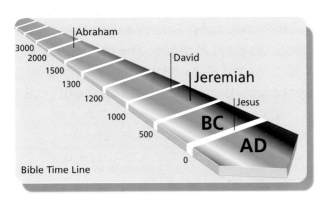

Bible Time Line

Abraham
3000
2000
1500
1300
1200
1000
500
David
Jeremiah
Jesus
BC
AD
0

to read it aloud in the Temple. Unlike him, Baruch wasn't barred. A crowd gathered as Baruch read the scroll. News of it soon reached the palace. King Jehoiakim listened to it and then destroyed the scroll, cutting off each section and throwing it into the fire. Jeremiah remembered how he'd sat down and dictated it all over again when he heard what had happened.

Darkness fell, but Jeremiah couldn't sleep. Vivid memories of the invasion by Nebuchadnezzar and his Babylonian army crowded into his mind. The disaster which he'd warned about had happened. Jerusalem was attacked. Jehoiakim was replaced by a new king, Zedekiah. The Babylonians were in charge. They invaded again, when Zedekiah refused to pay tribute to them. This time, with Egypt's help, Zedekiah forced them to retreat. There were massive celebrations, but when he continued to prophesy destruction by Babylon, Jeremiah's enemies accused him of undermining morale and threw him down the well to die.

You can read the full story in Jeremiah 19, 36–38

The silence was broken by the sound of voices. Ropes with some rags attached snaked down towards Jeremiah. He could hardly believe his eyes, but he quickly slipped the ropes under his arms. Four men pulled him steadily upwards. A servant in the palace had spoken up for him and had saved his life. The patch of sky grew bigger and then hands reached out and pulled him over the edge of the well. He'd survived and he could go on declaring his message. Only death would silence Jeremiah.

# The Heat of the Moment

King Nebuchadnezzar of Babylon glared at the three young men who stood before him. His orders had been crystal clear. They, along with his other officials, had come to the plain of Dura for the dedication of his statue. Like everyone else, they'd heard the herald's instructions to bow down to the statue as soon as the music started. They knew the penalty

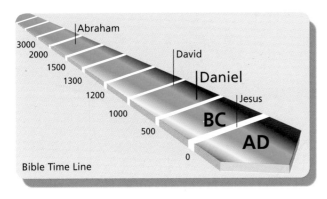

Bible Time Line

3000
2000
1500
1300
1200
1000
500
0
Abraham
David
Daniel
Jesus
BC
AD

for disobedience. Anyone who did not worship the statue would be burnt alive in a blazing furnace.

As soon as they heard the music, everyone bowed down and worshiped Nebuchadnezzar's statue apart from three men. Shadrach, Meshach and Abednego were dragged before Nebuchadnezzar. These were men who'd been taken captive when he'd attacked Jerusalem, trained for three years, given new names, and made members of his court. They owed him a lot, yet now, facing a terrible death,

they calmly told him they worshiped only one God, regardless of what was done to them.

Their cool, resolute reply made Nebuchadnezzar even more furious. He ordered the furnace to be heated to seven times its usual strength. The sweating laborers piled more fuel into the vast blazing furnace.

Meanwhile, Nebuchadnezzar commanded three of his strongest men to tie up Shadrach, Meshach and Abednego and throw them into the blazing furnace. As they hurled them into its fiery depths, the guards were hit by a solid wall of heat. They didn't survive. Shadrach, Meshach and Abednego fell into the heart of the flames.

Nebuchadnezzar stared at the sight before him. Instead of seeing three bodies being cremated, he saw four men walking around in the fire. They were not tied up and they didn't show any sign of being hurt by the flames. The king went as close to the furnace as he could bear and called Shadrach, Meshach and Abednego by name. They stepped out of the furnace. A huge crowd surged around them. Their hair wasn't singed, their clothes weren't burnt and they didn't even smell of smoke! Nebuchadnezzar's anger gave way to respect. They had risked their lives to obey their God. He decided to promote them and ordered that no one should ever speak disrespectfully of their God. Holding high office did not guarantee safety though, as Daniel, a close friend of Shadrach, Meshach and Abednego, was to discover for himself.

THE KING GOT IN A BLAZING TEMPER AFTER A HEATED DISCUSSION ABOUT SHADRACH, MESHACH & ABEDNEGO, BUT THEY KEPT THEIR COOL!

You can read the full story in Daniel 3

# Wild Cat Strike

The lions prowled around the bottom of the pit. They were angry at being confined in so small a space and very hungry. They looked up when they heard voices and saw a man being lowered towards them. As he fell in a heap on the earth floor, a large stone was pushed across the mouth of the pit. There was no way out.

King Darius watched as the stone was sealed to prevent any rescue attempts, then he walked back to his palace. He did not sleep that night. As he paced up and down, he grew more and more angry at the way in which he had been used to get rid of the one man he could trust absolutely. When Daniel

had arrived in Babylon with his friends Shadrach, Meshach and Abednego he'd proved to be such a good and honest servant that the king had chosen him and two other men to supervise the governors of his empire. Darius remembered how he'd considered putting Daniel in charge of the whole empire because his work was so outstanding. He hadn't realized that the other supervisors and governors had been trying to find something wrong with the way Daniel administered the empire but couldn't because he was so reliable and trustworthy. So when they came to him and suggested he should order the people not to request anything from anyone other than himself for thirty days on pain of death, he agreed. He just hadn't thought about what he was agreeing to. The next thing he knew was that Daniel's enemies were accusing him of breaking the law by praying to his God. They demanded that Daniel be arrested and thrown to the lions. That had only been a matter of hours ago, but already it seemed a lifetime.

Darius searched his memory again. Had he

I SEE WE HAVE DANIEL FOR DINNER!

MENU

I'M GLAD HE'S GOING. WE HAVEN'T HAD A BITE TO EAT FOR AGES!

done everything he could to rescue Daniel? For hours he tried to find a way to save Daniel's life but he couldn't. Daniel admitted that he knew about the new law and that he had broken it by refusing to stop praying to God every day. Darius was really upset, but there was no way out. The law had to be upheld.

Dawn broke and Darius rushed to the pit. His voice shook as he called Daniel's name. He wanted desperately to find him alive. The king was overjoyed when Daniel answered. God had saved him. The lions hadn't touched him. The stone was removed and Daniel was pulled out of the pit. Darius told him a new law would be passed ordering everyone to fear and respect the God who had protected him. Meanwhile, Daniel's enemies were arrested and tried. This time the lions did not go hungry.

You can read the full story in Daniel 6

# A Whale of a Time

The ship's captain had seen some unbelievable things in his time, but never before had he seen a fish swallow one of his passengers! Yet, in a way, he wasn't really surprised. It was all part of a strange voyage which began when a man called Jonah boarded the ship at Joppa. He had the look of a hunted animal but seemed to

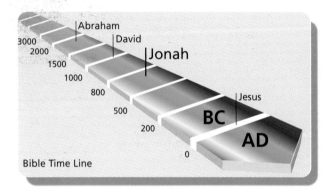

Bible Time Line

relax once he knew the ship was sailing to Spain.

They were far out to sea when the storm hit them. It was so violent that the sailors were terrified the ship would break up and they'd drown. While they were throwing the cargo overboard to lighten the load, the captain discovered Jonah fast asleep in the ship's hold. He was amazed that anyone could sleep when so many lives were in danger.

As the storm worsened, the superstitious sailors drew lots to find out who was to blame for the situation. Jonah's name was drawn and he admitted that he was trying to run away from God. He thought God wanted him to preach to the Assyrians, Israel's enemy. This was the last thing he wanted to do, so he tried to escape to Spain. But the escape plan failed and Jonah accepted that the storm must be all his fault. He offered to leap into the sea, but the crew didn't want him to die. They attempted instead to row to the shore, but it was hopeless. They gave up and took the only option they thought they had left. After praying for forgiveness, they threw Jonah overboard. Immediately the sea became calm, but while they were thanking God, they saw a huge fish rise out of the water and swallow Jonah whole.

# FISH FOOD

GULP!

Amazingly, Jonah survived. After some time inside the fish he was vomited onto dry land. He knew he deserved to die but his life had been spared. Jonah was so grateful that when God asked him to go to Nineveh again he set out right away to speak to his nation's enemies. His preaching was a great success. The people listened to him and believed God's message. They were willing to change their way of life and that made Jonah very, very angry. He didn't want them to repent and be forgiven by God. He wanted God to destroy them! He wanted God to love and care for him and his people only, not for people he regarded as his enemies. It took a long time and a lot of suffering before Jonah learned that his values were all wrong and that God has compassion for all people.

You can read the full story in Jonah 1–4

# THE GOOD NEWS

When Jesus was born, the Romans were in charge. The Jewish people hated being ruled by foreigners to whom they had to pay taxes. Some Jews wanted to use force to drive the Romans out but others tried to make the best of the situation.

John the Baptist always spoke the truth even when it was safer to keep quiet. It landed him in prison and eventually cost him his life. He was a powerful speaker who prepared the people for Jesus by telling all who came to listen to him that the long-awaited Messiah was coming. He told them they must change their ways and be baptized in the River Jordan to show they were making a fresh start.

Twelve men turned their backs on their homes and families to be Jesus' disciples and experience three years of excitement, danger, hardship and wonder. Wherever Jesus went large crowds gathered to hear him teach about God and see him heal the sick. Jesus was particularly concerned about the poor people and society's outcasts. He mixed happily with people who were labeled 'sinners'. This, and his preaching about the importance of living as God wants rather

than just sticking to the rules, made him many powerful enemies.

Jesus was betrayed by one of his disciples. He was arrested like a common criminal at night, put on trial, found to be innocent but sentenced to death because the Roman Governor was scared of riots and took the easy way out. Three days after his crucifixion and burial, Jesus rose from the dead. He appeared to his followers several times before he left them with the promise that he would send them the Holy Spirit.

The apostles became different people after they received the gift of the Holy Spirit. They stopped being scared and became fearless. They came out of hiding and maintained a high profile, preaching openly about Jesus. Stephen was stoned to death for insisting that Jesus was the Son of God. Among his killers was a man called Saul. He was proud of his reputation as the most successful persecutor of Christians. Then he encountered Jesus personally and became a changed man.

Saul, now known as Paul, felt compelled to spread the word about Jesus. He traveled far and wide, facing many hardships. His last journey was made under arrest to Rome. While he was under house arrest there, he wrote letters to the churches he'd helped set up. By the time he died, probably in A.D. 64, there were churches in all the main cities of the empire. Today there are Christians all over the world.

# A Child is Born

The shepherds were frozen to the spot. They were prepared for a sudden attack on their flocks by wild beasts but they were totally thrown by what they had just seen. It had started out as a routine night. They were carefully guarding their sheep on the hillside near Bethlehem as usual when an angel appeared with amazing news. Of all the people on earth, they were the first to be told that the Savior had been born. Then the angel was joined by a host of other angels singing God's praises. Just as suddenly, they disappeared. There was silence, and only the stars and the moon were visible in the clear night sky. Everything seemed the same as before the angel's appearance, but it wasn't. They agreed that the sheep must look after themselves while they made a personal visit to see the baby.

Mary was content. The difficult journey from Nazareth to Bethlehem, and the disappointment at finding nowhere to stay when she was so heavily pregnant, were just distant memories now. Her baby had been born, in a stable for sure, but all was well. Joseph could register for the census and then perhaps they could go home. It was a shock when the shepherds arrived and she was amazed

I'VE BEEN COUNTING ANGELS, BUT I JUST CAN'T GET TO SLEEP!

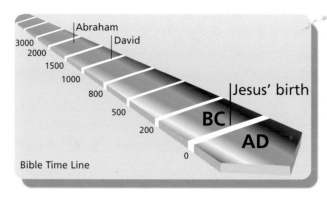

Bible Time Line

3000
2000
1500
1000
800
500
200
0
Abraham
David
Jesus' birth
BC
AD

when they told her what the angel had said about her child. The shepherds went back to work praising God because they'd seen their Savior. Mary thought long and hard about their visit. She had no idea that more unlikely visitors were on their way to see her baby.

Nothing would make the astrologers give up their quest. Ever since they'd seen the special star in the east they'd followed it, convinced it would lead them to a new king. It had led them towards Jerusalem, where they'd gone straight to the palace. Herod knew nothing about a new king. Nevertheless, he appeared enthusiastic about their search and sent them on to Bethlehem. They didn't realize that he had no intention of allowing anyone to rival him for the throne. He had decided to use them to find this new king so he could eliminate him!

At last the astrologers entered the house where Jesus was, bowed down and worshiped him and presented him with gifts of gold, frankincense and myrrh. They had intended going back to Jerusalem to tell Herod where Jesus was but they had a dream which changed their minds, and so they went home by a different route. Joseph had an important dream too. It made him decide to take Mary and Jesus over the border into Egypt. He was only just in time. Herod soon realized that the astrologers had given him the slip. He was furious and more determined than ever to kill this new king.

A STABLE FAMILY

You can read the full story in Luke 2; Matthew 2

# Preparing the Way

In the opinion of her family and the community, Elizabeth was a disgrace. Though she'd been married to Zechariah for a long time, she'd never had a child. When she grew too old for childbearing, she and Zechariah gave up hope of ever having a baby. Elizabeth was heartbroken. She believed she was a worthless failure.

Zechariah was a priest who took his duties seriously. He'd accepted the fact that he would never be a father but, one day while he was burning incense on the altar in the Temple, an angel appeared to him and told him that his prayers had been answered. It was such a shock to him that, for a moment, doubts crept in and he lost the ability to speak. He arrived home convinced that he and Elizabeth were going to have a really special son, but still unable to say a word.

Zechariah remained dumb until his son was eight days old and about to be named.

When Elizabeth discovered she was pregnant she was overcome with joy. Nobody could look down on her now, or make snide remarks behind her back. She still kept herself to herself though, so the first person to be told the news was Mary. To Elizabeth's surprise and delight, Mary visited her to share her own astounding news. She was going to have a baby too.

Elizabeth's son was born first. She was determined he should be called John, despite everyone else's insistence

HAVE I GOT NEWS FOR YOU!

that he should be named after his father. Zechariah backed her up, signaling for a writing tablet and writing on it, 'His name is John'. As soon as Zechariah had written it, his powers of speech returned. Friends and relations began to realize that this baby boy was different, and news of what was happening in Zechariah's family soon spread throughout Judea.

Years later, John left the comforts of home behind him and went to live alone in the desert. He wore simple clothes and existed on a diet of locusts and wild honey.

When he began preaching, people flocked to hear him. They traveled miles to be challenged by John, who didn't mince his words. He told them straight that they had to make an urgent and crucial decision to repent and be baptized. Then they had to show, by the way they lived, that they really had turned away from sin. But John had something more important than this to tell them. He was preparing the way for someone who was coming and who would change their lives for ever.

You can read the full story in Luke 1; Matthew 3

# All You Have to Do

John faced a real dilemma. Jesus wanted John to baptize him in the River Jordan like the others. John didn't like to refuse, but he knew that he wasn't good enough to undo Jesus' sandals, let alone baptize him. In the end he had to give in. Jesus insisted on identifying himself with the people so, after everyone else had been baptized, John went ahead and baptized him. While Jesus was praying, he heard God proclaim that he was his Son, the Messiah, who would suffer for his people and would save them. Jesus needed time to think. He left John and went alone into the wilderness to prepare himself for what lay ahead.

The wilderness certainly lived up to its name. It was wild and lonely and hardly anything grew there. Days passed, and having eaten nothing, Jesus became so hungry that he couldn't ignore it any longer. As he looked at the stones scattered across the dry desert floor, he imagined they could be loaves of bread. The Devil came to him and tempted him to use his power to turn the stones into bread and satisfy his hunger, but he rejected the temptation. Jesus knew that there were more important things in life than satisfying physical hunger.

Jesus moved on until he came to the top of a high mountain. He could see the landscape stretched out beneath him, reaching to the far horizons. The Devil offered to give him power over all he could see, if he worshiped him. But Jesus turned the whole idea down. He would worship God, and God alone.

The distance from the pinnacle of the Temple where Jesus stood to the bottom of the Kidron Valley below was mind-boggling. As he looked down at the ant-like figures of men and women, the Devil tempted Jesus to jump. God would ensure that he landed unhurt and

You can read the full story in Luke 4; Matthew 3, 14

then nobody would doubt that he really was God's Son. But Jesus didn't need to test God. He trusted him completely. Jesus went back to Galilee stronger and more certain than ever that he would trust and obey God in all things. He'd wrestled with temptation, but he hadn't given in.

News came that John had been arrested and imprisoned. Always outspoken, John had scolded Herod, the governor, for doing many evil deeds, including marrying his sister-in-law, Herodias. Herod wanted to kill him, but he spared his life because John was so popular with the people. Then, one night, everything got out of hand. Herod's stepdaughter danced for him at his birthday party and he was so pleased that he told her she could have anything she wanted. Herodias, the girl's mother, persuaded her to ask for John's head on a plate. An executioner was sent to the prison cell where John lay chained to the wall. A few minutes later a servant brought John's head to the king. John had always spoken the truth and he had paid for it with his life.

LEAD US NOT INTO TEMPTATION
BUT DELIVER US FROM EVIL
FOR YOURS IS THE KINGDOM
THE POWER AND THE GLORY

# Follow Your Leader

Crowds invaded the usually peaceful shore by Lake Gennesaret. Simon Peter kept well away from them. He had work to do. After a night's fishing, the nets needed washing so he got on with it. But when he looked up from his work, he saw that things were getting out of hand. Masses of people had followed Jesus onto the shore, desperate to hear what he had to say, but they were forcing him backwards into the water. Simon Peter held his boat steady as, under pressure from the crowds, Jesus climbed in. He asked the fisherman to push out from the shore so he could speak to the crowds from there. Simon Peter hauled the nets in and rowed out a few yards. After Jesus had finished speaking and the crowd had started to disperse, he told Peter to take the boat out into deeper water and let down the nets. Simon Peter didn't really want to. He and his partners, James and John, had fished all night and caught nothing and he was exhausted but there was something about Jesus that made him do what he was asked. He was in for a big surprise.

The nets broke under the weight of so many fish, and the boats were so full

ONE MORE FISH AND WE' WILL MAXIMISE OUR NET WORTH!

of fish that they were in danger of sinking. Simon Peter sank to his knees in front of Jesus. He knew he was in the presence of someone very special, someone who made him realize how unworthy he was. He was scared and James and John felt the same. They just wanted Jesus to leave, but he had other plans for them. When Jesus asked them to follow him, they didn't hesitate. They dragged their boats up on to the shore and walked away from the lives they'd always known.

Levi got up from his seat and walked away from his office and the life he'd always known. From the moment he'd started working as a tax collector, people had avoided him. He was hated because he worked for the Romans and, like all tax collectors, had a reputation for cheating people. But Jesus hadn't avoided him. Jesus had asked him to follow him and Levi just couldn't wait to celebrate. He threw a party, with Jesus as the guest of honor. Jesus shocked the religious leaders by going to the party and enjoying himself.

They couldn't believe that he would mix with people they regarded as undesirables. Jesus put them straight. His concern was for people like Levi and his friends, outcasts of society. The

CATCH YOU LATER!

religious leaders walked away disgusted. They didn't like what Jesus was doing. Somehow they'd have to find a way to stop him.

You can read the full story in Luke 5

# Feeling Better

While his friends kicked the roof in, the man lay helpless on a makeshift stretcher. Every square inch in the house below their feet was packed and there were more people outside pushing to get in. His friends had tried to force their way through the crowds but it was impossible, so they took the only remaining option. They made a hole and lowered him through the roof. The paralyzed man's view of the sky was replaced by a sea of faces as the stretcher gently bumped onto the ground at Jesus' feet.

Jesus was impressed by the men who'd been so determined that he should see their friend. He admired their faith and their concern for him. He looked at the man on the stretcher, then spoke to him. What he said left some

of the people in the crowd shocked and horrified.

The group of lawyers and Pharisees could hardly believe it. Jesus had just told the paralyzed man his sins were forgiven. This was blasphemy. As far as they were concerned, Jesus had no authority to forgive sins. Jesus knew what they were thinking and showed them he wasn't bluffing. Turning again to the man stretched out at his feet he

ROOF REPAIR FUND

Please give generously

told him to get up, pick up his bedroll and go home. Immediately the man stood, perfectly steady on his feet, bent to retrieve his bedroll, then set off for home and family praising God at the top of his voice. The people watched him go. They were awestruck. Never before had they seen anything like it...

Bartimaeus couldn't see a thing, but he could make a lot of noise. He screamed and yelled, ignoring the people around him who told him to keep quiet. Somewhere out there on the road was Jesus, the only person who could help him, and he was leaving the city. Shouting as loudly as he could, Bartimaeus pleaded with Jesus to take pity on him. Because he couldn't see Jesus stop and look in his direction, he just went on shouting and hoping, convinced that Jesus could heal him. Then he felt hands reach out for him, and people were telling him that Jesus wanted to talk to him.

It was so simple. Jesus asked him what he wanted. He said he wanted to see again. Jesus told him his faith had made him well. No sooner had he spoken, than Bartimaeus was able to

I HAVE SEEN THE LIGHT!

see. His eyes fixed on Jesus, he followed him down the road, thanking God all the time. The people watched him go. They were awestruck. Never before had they seen anything like it.

You can read the full story in Luke 5; Mark 10

# A Good Teacher

The disciples were stunned. While the crowds gathered nearby, Jesus sat with them on the mountainside and told them how they must make radical changes to the way they lived and thought. It was extraordinary. They knew the law, but Jesus said it wasn't enough to be good, law-abiding citizens. He expected more from them. He gave them examples that took them by surprise. He told them never to commit acts of violence, but he demanded much more—they must stifle the angry feelings which sparked off violence. The law allowed for retaliation, but Jesus urged them to show restraint in the face of aggression. To retaliate was to be no better than the aggressor. They had to be patient and prepared to mend broken relationships. All in all, Jesus asked them to behave better than the law demanded.

Jesus' teaching became even harder to accept and obey. He insisted that love was the bottom line, the basis on which they should treat one another. It was up to them to help others, but they should do so quietly and with the right motives, not just to boost their own self-esteem. They needed to remember that they weren't perfect and had no right to judge others. Most difficult of all, Jesus stressed

DO YOU THINK YOU MIGHT HAVE A BIT OF AN ATTITUDE PROBLEM?

that they must love their enemies. It was a revolutionary concept. They found it difficult to imagine a world in which people loved and prayed for their enemies.

By now Jesus was talking to the crowd which had gathered around him as well as to the disciples, and he had to make them realize that it was no good just listening to him and agreeing with him. They must put his teaching into practice in their own lives. Then, whatever life threw at them, they'd be able to stand firm. To help them understand, he told them a story about two men who had each built a house. One was wise and built his house on a rock. Even when it was battered by storms it stayed firm and secure, because it had solid foundations. This man was like the people who listened to Jesus and put what he said into practice. The other man, who represented those who heard Jesus' words but disregarded them, built his house on the sand. When the rain pelted down, the rivers overflowed and the gales blew, the outcome for him and his house was devastating.

You can read the full story in Matthew 5–7

83

# What a Welcome!

**S**imon was so disgusted he had to speak out. He'd invited Jesus to his home for a meal and it was being totally disrupted by an uninvited guest. The woman, a known prostitute, stood at Jesus' feet. She couldn't stop crying. As her tears fell on his feet, she wiped them away with her long hair. Then she kissed his feet and anointed them with the expensive perfume she'd brought with her. She clearly didn't care about what people thought.

Simon was completely thrown by the situation. It was so embarrassing. Jesus seemed to be completely unaware of the sort of person who was touching him. How could he let her come anywhere near him? Surely, as a prophet, he should know what a reputation she had.

Jesus knew precisely what was happening. He asked Simon a question. The answer was obvious. If a moneylender forgave one man a debt of five hundred silver pieces and another man a debt of fifty silver pieces, which of the two would be the most grateful? Jesus made his point: the more a person is forgiven, the more love he or she will show.

The woman left Simon's house feeling at peace. Jesus had not only told her that she was forgiven but he'd praised her for her devotion to him. He'd even reminded Simon that, although he'd been an adequate host, he'd not gone out of his way to give him a special welcome like the woman. Whatever the rest of the guests had thought about her, Jesus had understood and appreciated her actions.

TRESPASSERS
WILL BE
WELCOMED

Martha was so disgusted she had to speak out. She'd welcomed Jesus into her home and had gone immediately to prepare food for him. All the time she was working like mad, her sister, Mary, hadn't lifted a finger to help her. Instead, she'd sat herself down at Jesus' feet talking and listening to him. As she rushed around, Martha's feelings of resentment grew. The unfairness of it all got to her. If Jesus really cared about her he'd have noticed how she was struggling on her own while Mary did nothing. Martha couldn't keep quiet any longer. She turned on Jesus, but his reply shocked her. She was the one who had got her priorities wrong, not her sister. Mary had chosen to do what was most important—to take time to listen to Jesus.

You can read the full story in Luke 7, 10

85

# Popular Parables

He was safe at last. He'd thought he was a goner when he'd been mugged on the road from Jerusalem to Jericho. The muggers had been efficient and violent, robbing him of everything and leaving him battered and bleeding by the roadside. When a priest came along soon after, he thought everything was going to be all right, but the priest didn't even stop. He took one look, then crossed the road and walked past on the other side. A temple worker was his next hope and, sure enough, he came right up to him and looked at the state he was in. Then, to his amazement, he too crossed the road and walked on by. He would have died there, alone, if it hadn't been for the foreigner.

When the Samaritan saw the badly beaten man lying helpless by the road, he knew he had to do something. There was no love lost between Samaritans and Jews but that didn't stop him. He saw a man in desperate need and he felt for him. He gave him basic first aid, then lifted him onto his own donkey and took him to an inn. There he left him in the care of the innkeeper, paying him for his trouble in advance. He didn't forget the muggers' victim though. On his return journey, he stopped at the inn to find out how he was and to pay any extra costs.

Jesus paused at the end of the parable. He looked at the lawyer who'd asked him whom he should regard as

JERICHO   JERUSALEM

EE AW EE AW EE AW EE AW ...

his neighbor. Who, he asked him, had acted as a neighbor towards the man who'd been mugged? The lawyer admitted that the Samaritan had. Jesus told him he must show the same kind of loving concern to other people.

In another parable, Jesus described a family situation in which the father demonstrated love and forgiveness while his elder son showed no more care for his brother than the priest showed the victim in the parable of the good Samaritan.

The sound of music and dancing stopped the elder brother in his tracks. He called out to a servant to discover what was going on. When he heard that they were celebrating his younger brother's return, he was so angry he refused to enter the house. Ages ago his brother had waltzed off with his share of the inheritance and they'd not heard a word from him until now, when he'd turned up half-starved and in rags. He'd wasted a small fortune on having a good time, then, when he'd reached rock bottom, he'd come back home to ask his father to take him on as a servant. Instead, he'd been given a hero's welcome!

The boys' father left the party to try and persuade his eldest son to join in the celebrations, only to get a bitter response. His eldest son pointed out that nobody had ever thrown a party for him even though he was the eldest and had always been obedient and hard working. His father begged him to change his mind and welcome his brother home. All this time, he reminded him, they'd been scared that he might be dead, but he'd come home safe and sound.

You can read the full story in Luke 10, 15

# Naturally Miraculous

The disciples bailed the boat out as fast as they could, but it was a losing battle. When they'd set out, the water had been as flat as a pancake, but part way across the lake a storm had blown up. It was so fierce they were within minutes of sinking. The wind buffeted the boat, and waves broke over the sides. The disciples were terrified, but Jesus slept soundly in the back of the boat, totally oblivious to what was happening. With death staring them in the face, the disciples couldn't keep quiet any longer. They woke him up. Surely he cared whether they lived or died.

There was silence apart from the gentle lapping of the waves against the side of the boat. Jesus had said the word. Immediately the wind had died down and the water had become calm. He couldn't think why they'd been frightened, but the disciples were still very afraid. Who was this man? Even

the gale force wind and mountainous waves obeyed him!

It was another evening by Lake Galilee. Once again the disciples were faced with a problem, not life or death this time but one which they couldn't solve. A big crowd had followed Jesus around the lake and by sunset the people were hungry. Jesus was concerned about them but there were no shops nearby or money to buy food. Five thousand people needed feeding and they waited patiently and expectantly while Jesus discussed what could be done for them. The disciples had no ideas at all.

It took ages to pick up the leftovers. The disciples could scarcely comprehend what they'd just experienced. A boy had come forward and offered his food to Jesus. He'd gladly accepted it. Andrew had said what the rest of them were thinking: five bread rolls and two small fish wouldn't go far among so many thousands of people! Jesus ignored Andrew's comment. He thanked God for the food, then began to distribute it among the crowd. First he handed out the bread, then the fish. Everyone ate as much as they wanted. When the crowd had finally dispersed, the disciples were left with twelve baskets of breadcrumbs and plenty of food for thought!

You can read the full story in Mark 4; John 6

# Talking to God

He woke with a start. Someone was trying to break his door down. Then the shouting began and he recognized his next door neighbor's voice. He lay in bed listening to him making a major crisis out of having no food to give to an unexpected guest. The noise and disruption was about nothing more than borrowing some bread. It was infuriating. He shouted back that it was midnight, the door was locked, the family was asleep and he had no intention of getting up. The hammering on the door started up again but he told his neighbor, in no uncertain terms, to go away and leave him alone. The neighbor realized that their friendship wasn't going to be enough to get him out of bed, so he persisted in bashing on the door and shouting at the top of his voice. It worked. There was the sound of footsteps, the door opened and the bread was thrust into his hands.

Jesus explained to the disciples that just as the man in the parable kept on asking for what he needed, so they should be persistent in prayer, knowing that God would respond. Jesus told another parable to show that prayer should be sincere and not used as a means of showing off. He directed it particularly to one group of his listeners.

The Pharisee felt good about himself. He was not a greedy person. Never in his entire life had he been dishonest, and he had always stayed faithful to his wife. Then there was the religious side to his life. The law said people must fast once a year, but he fasted twice a week. The law said people must give a tenth of certain parts of their income, but he gave a tenth of all his income. He was quite something compared to other men, and he was proud of himself. He'd come to the Temple to pray but a tax collector was there too. The Pharisee made sure he didn't stand anywhere near him. He glanced at the man he regarded as scum and thanked God that he wasn't like him.

The tax collector felt lousy about himself. He didn't dare lift his eyes or hands to God in prayer. The memory of all the things he'd done wrong in his life flooded over him. There was nothing he could do but ask God to take pity on him.

You can read the full story in Luke 11, 18

Many of those listening to Jesus telling this story could relate to the Pharisee. They, too, were sure they were good, and despised people who they thought didn't come up to their standards. It was a terrible blow for them when Jesus rammed home the message that God accepted the tax collector's prayer because it came from the heart, but rejected the Pharisee's because he believed he was so good that he didn't really need God.

# Money Matters

He was a workaholic. His land was the most effectively farmed and the most productive in the area. Year by year he had to tear down his old barns and build bigger ones to store more grain and possessions. Whenever he found the pressure of work getting too much, he reminded himself of his master plan. He would work until he was stinking rich, then he'd sit back and do nothing but enjoy himself. The plan failed. One night after yet another grueling day, he dropped dead. Rich as he'd become, he never benefited from his money or his possessions. Jesus said the man was a fool. His whole attitude to life was fundamentally wrong. He believed possessions were all that really mattered, but they were no use to him when he was dead.

A young man with a similar attitude problem came to Jesus. He was rich, lived a good life and wanted to know what to do to receive eternal life. He talked to Jesus for a while, then, to the disciples' astonishment, he walked away dejectedly. He seemed to have

IF HE'S NOT CAREFUL, HE'LL WORK HIMSELF TO DEATH!

everything going for him but Jesus had asked him to take radical action. He'd asked him to sell everything and give the money to the poor. The rich young man couldn't do it. Just like the farmer, he put money first in his life. He couldn't square the promise of riches in heaven with cash in hand on earth, so he turned from Jesus and walked away.

The widow was as poor as the young man was rich. The only money she had amounted to two small copper coins, worth hardly anything. With no husband to support her, this was all she had to live on. Jesus sat near the Temple treasury and watched the people coming and going. Rich men paraded before it and made a great show of putting in large sums of money. Then the widow approached. She was a woman who'd sorted out the priorities in her life. For her, God always came first. Quietly and discreetly she dropped her coins into the treasury. Where God was concerned, she gave one hundred percent.

You can read the full story in Luke 12, 18, 21

# Branching Out

Zacchaeus' popularity rating in Jericho came way below that of the common slug. People looked down on Zacchaeus, not only because he was vertically challenged but because he was the chief tax collector. His job was a license to print money and Zacchaeus was very rich. He was hated and despised by everyone but he knew this was the price he had to pay for working for the Romans and getting rich on the backs of the poor.

Zacchaeus was among the masses of people who crowded the roadside when they heard that Jesus was going to pass through Jericho on his way to Jerusalem. Everyone wanted to catch a glimpse of him. Zacchaeus was interested in Jesus too. After all, he was known to be the friend of tax collectors, and tax collectors needed all the friends they could get! But Zacchaeus couldn't see over people's heads, and, being as popular as a sandstorm in a desert, no one would let him get to the front. So he climbed a tree, little realizing that his life was going to be changed forever.

Jesus looked up into the tree. When he saw Zacchaeus, he called him down and told him he was coming to his house. The people gasped with horror. They knew that Zacchaeus was a traitor and a cheat. They wouldn't touch him with a bargepole, so how come Jesus had chosen to visit him?

Zacchaeus felt about ten feet high! Out of everybody there, Jesus had chosen to speak to him and to stop by at his home. All his working life people had shunned him, had crossed the street when they saw him coming, but Jesus wanted to be his friend. It was an experience that brought out the best in Zacchaeus. After he'd welcomed Jesus, he told him he was going to be a totally different person from that moment on. He decided to give half of all he had to the poor and pay back those he'd cheated four times over. Like others who had come into contact with Jesus, Zacchaeus discovered that life would never be the same again.

HE'S PROBABLY LOOKING FOR TAX DODGERS!

You can read the full story in Luke 19

# A Warm Welcome

The kids thought it was brilliant. They shinnied up the palm trees and stripped the branches off them. Other children and adults spread the branches and items of clothing across the road. This was their way of greeting their ruler. A great roar went up as the procession approached the

city. First came a cheering crowd of Galileans. As their leader went past, the crowds by the roadside massed behind him. They followed him, praising God at the top of their voices. In the middle of it all, Jesus, who was the focus of their attention, sat astride a borrowed donkey.

The Pharisees standing among the crowds were not happy about this enthusiastic reception. They found it impossible to stand by and not protest. A group of them approached Jesus and told him to order his followers to be quiet. Jesus refused. What they were shouting was true. Their king had come. Jesus entered Jerusalem in triumph, but the mood soon changed when he visited the Temple.

It was chaotic. Animals were charging about all over the place, money-changers were scrabbling on the floor trying to retrieve their money, men were shouting, women and children were screaming. Jesus was in amongst the action overturning tables and driving the traders out of the Temple. They'd turned God's house, a place meant for prayer, into a den of thieves. They'd used every trick they knew to make as much money as they could from the worshipers and pilgrims who came there. Once Jesus had cleared them all out, he went back to the Temple every day to teach and heal the sick. Crowds of people turned up to see him. The authorities were furious.

They wanted Jesus dead but they didn't dare do anything because of his massive support among the ordinary people in Jerusalem.

Peter and John walked among the people through the narrow city streets. Jesus had sent them out to look for a most unusual sight—a man carrying a jar of water, something which was regarded as women's work. It was Passover time and the city was bursting at the seams, but they found the man. Without a word they followed him to a house. There the owner showed them a room where they could eat the Passover meal together.

The twelve disciples sat with Jesus around the table. This would be their last meal together before his suffering began. Jesus picked up some bread, broke it and said that his body was about to be given in death on their behalf. They should repeat this ceremony in remembrance of him. Later, he took a cup of wine saying that the wine symbolized his blood which would be spilt for them. While the disciples were still trying to take it all in, Jesus said something that totally threw them. He said that one of them was going to betray him.

You can read the full story in Luke 19, 22

# Betrayed by a Kiss

Judas had inside information and Jesus' enemies were prepared to pay for it. For thirty pieces of silver, Judas was willing to tell them when and where they could arrest Jesus without causing a riot.

Jesus did not want to die. Sadness overwhelmed him. That night he took the disciples to an olive orchard called Gethsemane, just outside the city boundary. He wanted his friends close by. He asked Peter, James and John to keep watch while he went a little further on. They didn't see him throw himself to the ground. They didn't hear him agonizing over the suffering which lay ahead. While Jesus wrestled with what was going to happen to him, Peter, James and John fell asleep.

Jesus walked over to the three men and woke them up. When he really needed them they'd let him down. He begged them to stay awake and pray. Tormented by his thoughts, Jesus still put God's will first, regardless of what it meant for him.

Meanwhile, the disciples had failed to stay awake, so he left them undisturbed. Peter, James and John were still sleeping when he finished praying. They didn't even stir at the noise made by Judas and the men sent by the chief priests and elders to arrest Jesus. As Jesus woke them up, they

THE PRICE

found themselves surrounded by a large crowd of armed men.

Judas walked straight up to Jesus and kissed him. This pre-arranged signal ensured there'd be no mistake about who to arrest in the dark garden. Men, armed with clubs and swords, closed in and held Jesus tight. The disciples were unprepared and outnumbered. They offered little more than token resistance. There was a bit of a commotion when one of them attacked

You can read the full story in Matthew 26

the High Priest's slave, severing his ear. Jesus told him to put away his weapon. There was to be no resistance. Events had to take their course, but it was he who was in charge of the situation, not Judas and the armed men. Coolly, Jesus pointed out that they could have arrested him at the Temple where he taught openly every day. Instead they'd chosen to come at night and take him as if he were an outlaw. By the time Jesus had finished speaking, his disciples had already turned tail and run.

# OF BETRAYAL

# Not Me

Peter's stomach churned. It was a nightmare. Only a short while ago he'd been in the garden of Gethsemane when Judas turned up with a crowd of armed men to arrest Jesus. He'd attacked a man who turned out to be the High Priest's servant but Jesus didn't want any violence so he'd put his sword away.

PETER TRIED TO KEEP A LOW PROFILE BUT …

When they started marching Jesus away, he ran off into hiding. He'd deserted Jesus, left him in the hands of his enemies, alone. Yet only hours before, during the Passover meal, he'd told Jesus he was willing to die for him.

Sure he'd followed them when they took Jesus away, but he'd hidden. He was so scared. And now he felt really vulnerable. He was sitting in the courtyard of the High Priest's residence where they'd taken Jesus. There were lots of other people sitting around the fire that had been lit in the center of the courtyard, but Peter felt as if everyone was looking at him. Then his worst fears were realized. One of the servant girls stared at him and commented loudly that she recognized him as one of the men who had been with Jesus. Peter glared back at her and protested violently that he didn't even know Jesus. He was the center of attention now, so he tried to hide

… HIS COVER WAS BLOWN AND …

his face. Gradually people returned to their own conversations and lost interest in him. Peter's pulse rate slowly stopped racing as he began to believe that he'd got away with it. It hadn't occurred to him that his Galilean accent was a dead give-away. Shortly afterwards, another person noticed him and remarked that he was one of Jesus' followers. Again Peter strongly denied it, but within the hour a man turned towards him and insisted that he was one of Jesus' close companions. Apart from anything else, he commented, it was blatantly obvious Peter came from Galilee.

... HE HAD TO MAKE A RUN FOR IT.

Peter was distraught. He felt like a cornered animal with nowhere to run. He told the man he didn't know what he was talking about, realizing as he said it how unconvincing it sounded. Then a rooster crowed, heralding the dawn. Jesus, who was held under heavy guard just a few yards away, turned around and looked straight at Peter.

Peter went cold. He remembered only too vividly Jesus telling him that he would deny him three times before the night was over. Peter broke down completely. He stumbled out of the courtyard, crying bitterly.

You can read the full story in Luke 22

# On Trial

Pilate, the Roman governor, received the Jewish delegation and their prisoner. Since they were not allowed to carry out the death sentence themselves, they had to convince Pilate that he should condemn this man to death. Immediately, they started

## CALL THIS JUSTICE?

BY OUR JERUSALEM CORRESPONDENT

### INNOCENT MAN CONDEMNED TO DEATH
### MURDERER SET FREE

The chief priests and members of the Council wanted Jesus dead. Thanks to Judas Iscariot, they had him in their power at last. They'd even overcome the lack of evidence against Jesus by bribing witnesses to lie about him. Their stories, though, didn't agree. In the rush to convict and kill Jesus there had been no time in which to rehearse the witnesses. The trial became such a fiasco that, finally, the High Priest stood up. He asked Jesus a direct question. Was he the Messiah, the Son of God? With simple dignity, Jesus affirmed that he was. The High Priest tore his robes. He could hardly disguise his grim satisfaction. There was no need for any more witnesses. Jesus had condemned himself. The vote was unanimous. Jesus must die.

accusing Jesus of treasonous activities. Jesus said nothing. Pilate could see he'd been roughed up and was impressed by his grave silence. On the other hand the governor was unconvinced by the torrent of accusation and said as much. The chief priests and crowds erupted into even stronger protests. They could see the situation slipping out of their control, so they picked on something which they thought would worry Pilate.

MY VERDICT IS NOT GUILTY SO I'M SENTENCING HIM TO DEATH!

They told him that Jesus' teaching would result in riots and that he'd already started stirring up trouble in Galilee. Pilate grabbed the opportunity to offload the problem of what to do with Jesus on to Herod, the ruler of Galilee.

Herod was pleased. He'd heard about Jesus and he particularly wanted to watch him perform a miracle. Jesus had nothing to say to Herod. He met every question with silence. Once again the chief priests and lawyers made their accusations against Jesus. Herod was disappointed and frustrated by Jesus' attitude towards him. He joined his soldiers in making fun of Jesus, then sent him back to Pilate.

Pilate delivered his verdict. Jesus was not guilty of any of the crimes he'd been accused of. He certainly didn't deserve to die, so he sentenced him to be whipped, then set free. There was uproar. The crowd, wound up by the priests, demanded that Barabbas, a well-known revolutionary, be released instead. Pilate wasn't too happy about letting a dangerous man loose, but the crowd was insistent. After appealing to the people for the third time, Pilate decided it was wiser to give in to them.

He ordered the release of Barabbas, a rioter and murderer, and handed Jesus over to be crucified.

You can read the full story in Mark 14; Luke 23

# Christ Crucified

The soldiers threw dice as three men hung dying on rough wooden crosses. The winner got first pick of the clothes they'd taken off Jesus, the one being crucified between two thieves. They'd stripped Jesus of his outer clothes earlier when they'd used him in an impromptu theatrical play. Everyone in Pilate's palace who'd been watching had had a right good laugh. They'd slung a red cloak around Jesus' shoulders, made a crown out of thorn

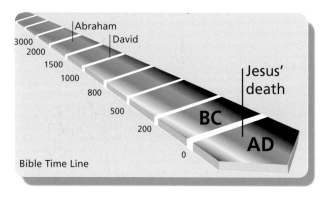

Bible Time Line

branches, stuck it on his head and put a stick in his hand, then bowed mockingly before him and called him the King of the Jews. It turned a bit nasty after that. Some of them started spitting at him and hitting him. Then they took him to Golgotha, the place of execution.

Having sorted out who was having which item of clothing, the soldiers watched Jesus die. They nailed a notice at the top of his cross: 'This is Jesus,

the King of the Jews'. Passers-by teased him, saying that if he was the Son of God, why didn't he save himself. They shouted to him to climb down off the cross, then they'd believe in him. Even the criminals suffering each side of him joined in with the taunts and insults.

The morning wore on. A small group of people, including Jesus' mother and some of his friends, kept vigil at the foot of the cross. The soldiers waited patiently. They were used to crucifixion duty. The victims took hours to die. Suddenly, at midday, when the sun should have been at its hottest and brightest, everything went dark. It stayed that way for three hours.

Jesus cried out, startling the soldiers and prompting one of the bystanders to soak a sponge in some wine and offer it to him. Soon afterwards, Jesus gave another loud cry and died. The earth shook, rocks split apart, graves opened, dead people were raised to life.

The soldiers stood transfixed. They'd witnessed the sun's light being blotted out and heard Jesus' cry break the uncanny silence. They'd felt and seen the effects of the earthquake after Jesus had taken his last breath. Terrified, they turned to one another, as they realized who they had just crucified—the Son of God.

You can read the full story in Matthew 27

# The Empty Tomb

When Pilate handed Jesus over to be crucified, he thought he'd heard the last of him. He couldn't have been more wrong. That very evening he was taken aback when a wealthy man, Joseph from Arimathea, approached him and asked if he could have Jesus' body. He wanted to bury Him in his tomb before the Sabbath began. Usually people executed for treason were thrown into a common grave but, at the time, Pilate was quite happy to hand the body over. His involvement with Jesus of Galilee still wasn't over though.

On the Sabbath day, a delegation of chief priests and Pharisees arrived. They told Pilate about Jesus' prediction that he would rise again after three days and insisted that a guard be

placed by the tomb. Pilate didn't need any persuasion. If the body came up missing and Jesus' followers told everyone he had been raised from the dead, then anything might happen and he might not be able to control the situation. With his full co-operation, they blocked the entrance to the tomb

FIRST JUDAS, THEN THE TRIAL WITNESSES, NOW THE GUARDS ..... THIS BRIBERY'S AN EXPENSIVE BUSINESS!!

with a stone and left soldiers on guard around the clock.

It was still dark the following morning when Mary Magdalene visited the tomb, but there was enough light to see that the stone had been rolled away. Mary ran to tell the disciples that the grave had been robbed. She found Simon Peter and one of the other disciples and told them what had happened. They were on their way before she'd even finished giving them the news. Peter went into the empty tomb and saw the linen wrappings lying there. The other disciple checked it out too, then they returned home. Mary remained alone outside the tomb, crying as if her heart would break. She was still convinced that someone had stolen Jesus' body.

The chief priests were in a real panic. After three days the stone had been moved and Jesus' body had gone. They had to arrange some sort of cover-up. In exchange for a very large bribe the soldiers who'd been on guard agreed to lie and say that they had fallen asleep. While they were sleeping Jesus' body had been stolen.

Mary turned around. A man was standing near her but, blinded by her tears, she didn't recognize him. She thought he was the gardener and asked him if he was responsible for taking away Jesus' body. Then he said her name. Mary couldn't fail to recognize Jesus' voice. Joy and relief flooded over her. Jesus told her to go back to the disciples and tell them that he was returning to his Father, God. Once again Mary ran to the disciples, but with a very different message this time—the message that Jesus had risen from the dead!

You can read the full story in Matthew 27, 28; John 20

# No Doubt About It

Thomas had his doubts. He hadn't been around when Jesus appeared to the other disciples late on the Sunday evening. He listened intently to their description of how Jesus had suddenly appeared amongst them as they sat behind locked doors, scared of being arrested by the Jewish authorities. Strangely, he didn't make any comments or ask any questions when they related to him what Jesus had said to them that night. As far as Thomas was concerned, it was great that they were so thrilled about what had happened, but he was adamant. Unless he could see and touch Jesus' scarred and wounded body then, regardless of what they said, he wouldn't believe he'd risen from the dead.

A week passed. Thomas joined the others in hiding. Just as suddenly as before, Jesus appeared among them. Thomas felt as though Jesus knew all about his doubts and was there just for him. Jesus showed him the marks of the nails in his hands and the gash in his side where one of the soldiers had plunged his spear. He told him to stop doubting and believe. Thomas needed no more proof. He had no more doubts. Jesus, who had been crucified, dead and buried, was alive.

PROOF POSITIVE

The next time Thomas saw Jesus was at an early morning barbecue on the shore of Lake Tiberias. He and the other disciples had left Jerusalem and gone to Galilee. When Peter suggested to some of them that they should go fishing, they thought it was a good idea. By the time they'd fished all night and caught nothing, they'd changed their minds. As the sky lightened, they were just able to make out a figure standing at the water's edge. They didn't know who he was, but they obeyed when he shouted instructions across the water to cast their net on the right side of the boat. When they tried to haul the net in, it proved impossible. The weight of the fish they'd caught was too great. One of the disciples in the boat figured out that the mystery man was Jesus. He told Peter, who couldn't wait to be with him. Pulling his cloak around him, Peter jumped into the water and swam straight for Jesus, leaving Thomas and the others to row for shore.

They had a strange yet wonderful meal on the beach that morning. They cooked some of the freshly caught fish over a campfire and ate it with bread. Jesus handed the food around. It wasn't

You can read the full story in John 20, 21; Acts 1

the last time they saw and talked with him. Jesus appeared to them many more times, and before he finally returned to heaven he promised that something very powerful and remarkable was going to happen to them.

I THINK WE MUST BE THE ONLY FISH LEFT IN THE LAKE!

# Bubbling Over

Suddenly Jesus' followers fell silent and listened. A strange noise, like a strong wind, filled the room where they'd gathered. Moments later, they saw what looked like tongues of fire spreading out and touching each one of them. They started talking again, but this time in different languages. Jesus' promise had come true. Something very powerful and remarkable had happened to them. The Holy Spirit was with them.

The noise they were making attracted a large crowd. It was the festival of Pentecost and Jerusalem was packed with Jewish visitors from other countries. Excitement mounted as these visitors heard their own language being spoken. They looked with amazement at these believers from Galilee who were able to communicate with Jews and Gentiles from all over the known world. A few sceptics in the crowd reckoned they were drunk.

**FROM**

**FROM**

**LIVES TRANSFORMED**

# TO

# TO

begged them for some money. But he got more than he bargained for. Peter had no money to give the man but he had something far better. Stretching out a helping hand he told him, in Jesus' name, to stand up and walk.

Without any hesitation, the man leapt to his feet and walked around marveling at this new experience. Holding on to Peter and John he entered the Temple. He walked and jumped and praised God at the top of his voice. He just couldn't stop celebrating.

They soon understood. Peter, who only a few years ago had been a simple fisherman, stood up and addressed the huge crowd. After he'd finished speaking, three thousand people joined the ever-growing number of believers. On their way to the Temple Peter and John saw a lame man sitting by the Beautiful Gate. He

Everyone turned around to look at him. When they recognized the man they'd only known as a lame beggar, they could scarcely believe their eyes. A crowd soon gathered and Peter felt he had to explain what had happened. It was a dangerous thing to do. Peter was still talking when the priests arrived with the Temple guards. They immediately arrested both him and John and threw them into prison.

You can read the full story in Acts 2–4

# Bitter Persecution

Peter and John refused to be intimidated. The day after their arrest, the Council ordered them never to speak of Jesus again but they calmly replied that it was impossible.

The Council couldn't do anything to them. Too many people knew about the miracle of the lame man and wanted to hear the news about Jesus. If they dared to punish Peter and John they'd be the

target for a tremendous popular backlash. When Peter and John were freed, the Council members admitted that they'd been beaten this time, but they weren't finished yet.

Peter looked around his cell. With its bare stone walls and solid door that was locked and bolted, it was basic but secure. Outside, Peter knew, there'd be men on guard. Being thrown into prison was becoming a familiar experience for

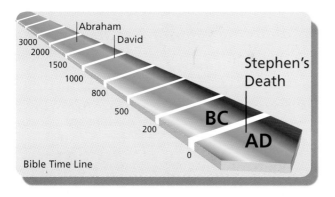

Bible Time Line

him and the others. This time a handful of them had been arrested. The Jewish leaders had to do something about the increasing number of believers. The following morning the Temple officers arrived at the jail to question Peter and the others. The jail was securely locked and the guards were standing at the doors but there was no one inside. During the night the apostles had discovered that their cell doors were open and they'd walked out. Despite being rearrested, interrogated and whipped, Peter and the other apostles continued to preach and teach every day. More and more people joined them, but life for the believers became increasingly dangerous.

Stephen was seized without warning and taken before the Council. A close friend of the twelve apostles, he'd never been afraid to speak out in public about Jesus. It had made him many enemies. As he stood before the Council members, men came forward and told lies about him. They'd been bribed and Stephen ignored them. He told the truth but the truth hurt. The Council members ground their teeth in anger, but when Stephen spoke of seeing Jesus standing beside God, they went berserk. They couldn't wait for a trial, but dragged Stephen out of the city and began to stone him.

Stephen went down under a particularly vicious barrage of stones, but they didn't stop. They continued venting their anger and frustration on him. As Stephen died, praying for forgiveness for his murderers, a young man called Saul looked on. It felt good to see a well-known Christian silenced. Then and there he decided to take the lead in destroying more believers. He built a reputation for himself as the most successful persecutor of Christians ever. Then, in the middle of his anti-Christian campaign, he made a fateful journey to Damascus.

You can read the full story in Acts 4–7

# A Change of Heart

The light shone straight into his eyes and Saul collapsed. As he lay on the ground, unable to see a thing, he heard Jesus' voice asking why he was persecuting him. His companions on the journey to Damascus heard the voice too but weren't affected by the flash of light. Saul got to his feet carefully. He couldn't see. Feeling totally helpless, he had to be led by the hand into Damascus, the city in which he'd intended to hunt down every Christian. Three days later Saul was still blind and refusing to eat or drink.

Ananias had heard all about Saul's obsession with destroying Christians. He knew he and the other believers living in Damascus were next on Saul's hit list. That frightened him, but he was terrified when he had a vision telling him to go to Judas' house in Straight Street and heal Saul who had gone blind. Saul was the last person on earth Ananias wanted to meet yet, scared as he was, he set out for the house believing that God had chosen Saul to serve him.

YOU GO HOME. THERE'S NO WAY SAUL CAN ESCAPE TONIGHT.

Saul heard someone enter the house and turned his head in the direction of the sound. Ananias explained why he was there. Saul felt Ananias' hands on him and it was as if scales fell from his eyes. His sight came back immediately and completely. He could see as clearly as before that blinding light on the road to Damascus. Full of relief and joy and his new faith, Saul was baptized. Within a day or so, the man who had found fame as the most successful persecutor

You can read the full story in Acts 9

of Christians ever, was preaching in the synagogues of Damascus that Jesus was the Son of God.

People were baffled. Saul was famous for killing everyone who worshiped Jesus. He'd come to Damascus to find some more victims, yet here he was insisting that Jesus was the Messiah. Saul was a powerful preacher and his arguments were very convincing.

As the days passed, the Jews became increasingly concerned. They had to organize themselves and stop him preaching. They planned to treat Saul the same way that he'd always treated Christians. They would kill him.

It was the dead of night but Saul's enemies were keeping a round-the-clock watch on the city gates. They were determined he wouldn't get away. They didn't see the basket being lowered down the outside of the city walls on a rope. As soon as it hit the ground Saul climbed out and waved a silent farewell to his friends. He'd escaped from Damascus unharmed. He set off to join the disciples in Jerusalem. If he thought they'd welcome him with open arms, he was very much mistaken.

# On the Road

The apostles in Jerusalem refused to believe that Saul was a Christian. His very name sent a chill down their spines. It was Barnabas who finally got them to accept him. He told them what had happened to Saul on his way to Damascus and how courageously he had preached there.

Barnabas and Paul, as Saul became known, made a great team. They set out together to spread the good news about Jesus. It was the beginning of many years of traveling for Paul. He succeeded in founding many new Christian communities but he had to face terrible dangers.

Huge numbers flocked to listen to Paul and Barnabas preach in Iconium. Among the crowd were those who violently disagreed with what they said about Jesus, yet the more they voiced their opposition, the more outspoken Paul and Barnabas became. The only answer was to silence them. They decided to beat them up and stone them, but before they could carry out their drastic plan, Paul and Barnabas fled to Lystra.

The excitement in Lystra was electric. Crowds of people had just seen Paul heal a man who'd been lame from birth. It was obvious that Paul and Barnabas were gods who had become men. They gave them the names of gods and prepared to offer sacrifices to them. Paul and Barnabas were horrified. They ran into the middle of the crowd, protesting that they were only human and just wanted to tell them about the living God. The people paused for a moment, but they still wanted to offer a sacrifice to them. When Paul and Barnabas' enemies from Iconium arrived, they succeeded in turning the crowd against them. Reverence for the two men turned to hatred. Stones and rocks started to fly. Paul fell to the ground and lay very still.

Paul survived. Both he and Barnabas went back to the places where they'd been rejected and they visited other towns and cities. Paul's adventures had just begun.

You can read the full story in Acts 9, 14

# Second Time Around

The girl was a little goldmine. Her behavior might be peculiar but the customers loved her. She was the most sought after fortune-teller in Philippi and, because she was a slave, every penny she earned went straight to her owners. Then two Christians, Paul and Silas, arrived in town. The girl started following them around and shouting after them. It happened day after day and it was obvious that it was getting to Paul. One day, he suddenly turned around and ordered the evil spirit which possessed her to leave her. She was cured instantly and lost her ability to predict the future. Now her owners would never make a fortune from her. They were very angry, bitter men and they wanted revenge.

Grabbing hold of Paul and Silas they dragged them before the Roman officials in Philippi's public square. They accused them of causing trouble in the city, an accusation guaranteed to upset the Roman authorities. With the crowd joining in the attack, Paul and Silas didn't stand a chance. They were stripped, badly beaten and thrown into prison.

The jailer drew his sword. He prepared to kill himself. The Roman officials had insisted that he guard Paul and Silas very closely when they were handed over to him. He'd taken every

I DON'T BELIEVE IT! SHE'S FOUND HER MIND AND WE'VE LOST A FORTUNE!

PRISONERS
## PAUL & SILAS
OFFENSE
## MAKING TROUBLE
CELL BY DATE
50AD

precaution, locking them up in an inner cell with their feet fastened between heavy blocks of wood. How could he have known that there'd be a violent earthquake during the night, and that all the cell doors would fly open and everybody's chains come loose? All his prisoners must have escaped. He'd pay for it with his life and he preferred to die by his own hand.

Someone shouting stopped him. He put his sword down and sent for a light. Paul, Silas and all the other prisoners were still there. They could have walked out, but they'd stayed in jail. The jailer couldn't believe it. He led Paul and Silas out of their cell and begged them to tell him what he should do to be saved. By the next morning he and his family had been baptized and the Roman authorities had decided to let Paul and Silas go free.

Paul refused to leave. The officials felt humiliated but scared too. They'd discovered that Paul and Silas were Roman citizens. They went to the jail, apologized, let them out and then asked them politely to go on their way. Paul and Silas left Philippi. For once justice had been done.

You can read the full story in Acts 16

# The Last Journey

The ship's captain made a near fatal mistake. He decided to leave a safe harbour and sail to a more sheltered one. Paul advised against it, but the captain wouldn't listen. Paul was just one of several prisoners on board being transported under armed guard to Rome. Once out to sea, there was a gentle sea breeze. The captain was sure he'd made the right decision. Before long though, it became a hurricane force wind. The storm continued day and night. The captain tried everything from having the cargo

276 MEN OVERBOARD

thrown overboard to lowering the anchor. The situation was desperate. Day after day the storm raged with no sign of easing up. Although he didn't

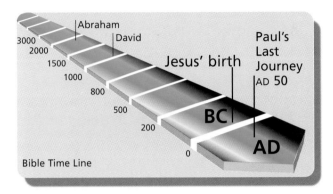

Abraham
David
Jesus' birth
Paul's Last Journey
AD 50
3000
2000
1500
1000
800
500
200
0
BC
AD
Bible Time Line

say it out loud, the captain thought the same as the crew—they were all going to die.

Paul tried to encourage the crew and his fellow prisoners. He told everyone who would listen that they weren't going to die. Only the ship would be lost, not their lives. They had to look after themselves and trust in God. It always worked for him.

Never having been afraid to look danger in the face, Paul found himself a prisoner on a sinking ship because he'd ignored his friends' warnings. He'd gone to Jerusalem and taught in the Temple and caused a riot. The mob had tried to kill him but he'd been rescued just in time. With his enemies still determined to kill him, Paul appealed to Rome, and the authorities decided to send him to be tried before Caesar.

At midnight, two weeks later, the crew suspected that the ship was close to land. They dropped four anchors,

afraid that the ship would be wrecked on the rocks in the darkness. As dawn broke, they saw a sandy bay and decided to run the ship aground. They cut the anchors, raised the mainsail and hit a sandbank. With the prow of the ship stuck fast, the stern started to break up under the force of the waves.

The soldiers drew their swords. This was the end for the prisoners. There was no way they were going to be given the chance of swimming ashore and escaping. It was their officer who stopped the massacre. He wanted to keep Paul alive, so it was agreed that all who could swim should jump overboard and make for shore while the others followed, hanging on to planks of wood. Everyone reached the shore safely. They were on the island of Malta, and there they stayed for the next three months.

There was a warm welcome awaiting Paul in Rome. People traveled for miles to see him. Kept under strict house arrest, Paul used his time to write many letters to the churches in the towns and cities he'd visited over the years and to preach to anyone within earshot. For Paul, the end was near, but for the Christian church it was only the beginning.

You can read the full story in Acts 27, 28

121

# WHO'S WHO

**Aaron** Moses' brother and spokesman.

**Abednego** Abednego, Shadrach and Meshach were exiled to Babylon with Daniel. The three companions refused to bow down to Nebuchadnezzar's statue and were thrown into the fiery furnace. They survived unharmed.

**Abigail** Nabal's wife, who persuaded David not to take revenge on her husband. Married David after Nabal died.

**Abraham** Father of the nation of Israel. He always put God first in his life.

**Absalom** Son of David. Led a revolt against his father. Killed by Joab when fleeing from the battlefield.

**Ahab** King of Israel who seized Naboth's vineyard. Married to Jezebel. An opponent of Elijah, he allowed the people to worship Baal. A weak, selfish man. He died in battle.

**Ammon** Son of David. Killed by Absalom.

**Ananias** Christian living in Damascus sent to Saul to restore his sight.

**Andrew** Peter's brother. A fisherman. One of the twelve disciples.

**Barabbas** A revolutionary released instead of Jesus.

**Barak** Commanded Israelite army in battle against Sisera.

**Barnabas** Accompanied Paul on one of his missionary journeys.

**Bartimaeus** Blind man whose sight was restored by Jesus.

**Baruch** Jeremiah's secretary and friend. Wrote down all Jeremiah dictated on a scroll and read it aloud in the Temple.

**Bathsheba** Wife of Uriah. David committed adultery with her and later married her. Mother of Solomon.

**Benjamin** Jacob's youngest son. Rachel died giving birth to him.

**Boaz** Related to Naomi. A rich Bethlehem landowner he was impressed by the hard working, caring Ruth and married her.

**Daniel** Taken captive to Babylon as a young man and trained for service at court. Honest and trustworthy, he remained loyal to God. Was thrown to the lions but was unhurt.

**Darius** King of Babylon who passed a law which resulted in Daniel being thrown into a pit of lions.

**David** Youngest son of Jesse. A shepherd boy and talented musician. A hero to the people after he killed Goliath. Spent years as an outlaw because of Saul's jealousy. After Saul's death, he became Israel's second king.

**Deborah** Prophetess at the time of the Judges. She encouraged Barak to overthrow Sisera.

**Delilah** Philistine woman who betrayed her husband, Samson, for money.

**Eli** Priest at Shiloh. He looked after and trained Samuel.

**Elijah** One of Israel's greatest prophets. Had contest with prophets of Baal.

**Elkanah** Husband of Hannah and Peninnah. Samuel's father. A kind and caring man.

**Elimelech** Naomi's husband. He died in Moab.

**Elisha** Elijah's successor as prophet of Israel.

**Elizabeth** Married to Zechariah and mother of John the Baptist. Visited by her cousin Mary when they were both pregnant.

**Esau** Son of Isaac and Rebecca, twin brother of Jacob. Exchanged his birthright for some food and was cheated of his blessing by Jacob.

**Esther** Young Jewish exile chosen to be Xerxes' queen. Brave and determined, she saved her people from being massacred.

**Gehazi** Elisha's servant. Lied in order to steal presents Naaman offered to Elisha. He suffered a terrible punishment for this.

**Gideon** Defeated the Midianite army with only three hundred men during the time of the Judges.

**Goliath** Gigantic Philistine champion. Scornful of David who took up his challenge but was killed by a single sling shot.

**Haman** Xerxes' Prime Minister. Hated Mordecai and plotted against the Jews. A resentful, vindictive man, he was hanged on the gallows he'd built for Mordecai.

**Hannah** Wife of Elkanah. Dedicated her first child, Samuel, to God's service.

**Herod the Great** Ruler of Judea when Jesus was born. After news that a new king had been born he thought his position of power might be threatened, so he ordered the killing of all the baby boys in Bethlehem.

**Herod Antipas** Son of Herod the Great. Married Herodias. Had John the Baptist imprisoned and executed. Pilate sent Jesus to him when he was on trial.

**Herodias** Wife of Herod Antipas. Told Salome to ask for John the Baptist's head.

**Isaac** Son of Abraham and father of Jacob and Esau.

**Jabin** King of Hazor in time of Judges. Cruel, violent enemy of Israelite people.

**Jacob** Son of Isaac. Clever and devious, he cheated his brother Esau out of his inheritance. Jacob became the father of twelve sons.

**Jael** Killed Sisera with a tent-peg.

**James** Brother of John. Fisherman in partnership with Peter. One of the twelve disciples.

**Jehoiakim** King who burnt Jeremiah's scroll of prophecies.

**Jehu** King of Israel. Drove his chariot over Jezebel's body after she'd been thrown from a window.

**Jeremiah** Great prophet of Judah at the time of its fall to Babylon. Made many enemies because he told people what they didn't want to hear.

**Jesse** Father of eight sons, the youngest being David. Grandson of Ruth and Boaz.

**Jethro** Moses' father-in-law.

**Jezebel** Wife of Ahab who promoted Baal worship in Israel. Cruel, scheming woman who had no conscience. She hated Elijah. Responsible for Naboth's death. Thrown to her death on Jehu's orders.

**Joab** David's nephew and commander of his army. Killed David's son, Absalom.

**John the Baptist** Son of Elizabeth and Zechariah. Lived alone in the desert for years, then began preaching and preparing the people for Jesus' coming. His outspokenness made him powerful enemies. Executed on the orders of Herod.

**John** Brother of James. One of the twelve disciples.

**Jonah** Prophet with a mission to Nineveh. Tried to get out of it and was swallowed by an enormous fish. Had to obey God in the end.

**Jonathan** Eldest son of Saul, close friend of David. Killed in battle alongside his father.

**Joseph** Jacob's favorite son, hated by his brothers who sold him into slavery. Seemingly spoiled and boastful as a youngster, he proved to be honest, responsible and a man of God. He became second-in-command to the king in Egypt.

**Joseph** Carpenter from Nazareth, married to Mary, Jesus' mother.

**Joseph of Arimathea** Wealthy man who asked Pilate for Jesus' body and placed him in his own tomb.

**Joshua** Succeeded Moses as leader of Israel. Responsible for leading the people into the Promised Land.

**Judah** One of Jacob's twelve sons. He was prepared to be punished in place of Benjamin.

**Judas Iscariot** One of the twelve disciples. He betrayed Jesus for thirty pieces of silver. Later, he committed suicide.

**Laban** Rebecca's brother and Jacob's uncle who made him experience what it was like to be the victim of cheating.

**Leah** Elder daughter of Laban. Jacob's wife and mother of six of his sons. Jacob was conned into marrying Leah and never loved her.

**Levi** Tax collector who became one of the twelve disciples.

**Lot** Abraham's nephew who chose to live in Sodom and narrowly escaped death.

**Martha** Sister of Mary. Close friend of Jesus. Upset when Jesus visited and she did all the work while her sister sat and talked to Jesus.

**Mary** She and her sister Martha were close friends of Jesus.

**Mary** The mother of Jesus and wife of Joseph.

**Mary Magdalene** The first person to see Jesus after his resurrection.

**Merab** Saul's daughter, promised in marriage to David but given to another man.

**Meshach** *See* **Abednego**.

**Michal** Saul's daughter. Married to David. Helped him escape when her father was trying to kill him.

**Mordecai** Esther's cousin. He uncovered a plot to assassinate Xerxes and encouraged Esther to save her people from massacre.

**Moses** Adopted by an Egyptian princess, his hatred of injustice and impetuosity got him into trouble. He became a great leader and law-giver and led his people out of slavery.

**Naaman** Syrian army commander who suffered from leprosy. Visited Elisha and was cured after bathing in the River Jordan.

**Nabal** Rich man, married to Abigail. Mean and bad tempered, he refused to provide David's men with food. Collapsed and died after a drinking bout.

**Naboth** Owner of a vineyard Ahab wanted. Refused to sell, so Jezebel engineered his death.

**Naomi** Woman from Judah who went to live in Moab but returned to Bethlehem after her husband and sons died. Mother-in-law of Ruth and Orpah.

**Nathan** Prophet who visited David and made him see the error of his ways in the Uriah/Bathsheba affair.

**Nebuchadnezzar** King of Babylon who captured Jerusalem and took the Judeans into exile. Ordered Shadrach, Meshach and Abednego into the fiery furnace when they refused to bow down to his statue.

**Obed** Ruth and Boaz' son.

**Orpah** Naomi's Moabite daughter-in-law who returned to her parents when Naomi went back to Bethlehem.

**Paul** Watched Stephen die. Was the foremost persecutor of Christians until a personal encounter with Jesus on the road to Damascus. Despite many hardships, traveled far and wide telling people the good news about Jesus.

**Peninnah** Elkanah's second wife. Cruelly taunted Hannah during the years when she was childless.

**Peter** Fisherman. Brother of Andrew. One of the twelve disciples.

**Pilate** Roman Governor who ordered the crucifixion of Jesus although he knew he had done nothing wrong.

**Potiphar** Officer of Pharaoh in whose household Joseph served.

**Rachel** Laban's daughter. Jacob's favorite wife and mother of Joseph and Benjamin. Died giving birth to Benjamin.

**Rahab** Woman living in Jericho who hid two Israelite spies and helped them escape from the city.

**Rebecca** Wife of Isaac. Mother of twins, Esau and Jacob. She doted on Jacob.

**Reuben** Eldest of Jacob's twelve sons who tried to save Joseph from his brothers' plan to murder him.

**Ruth** Naomi's Moabite daughter-in-law who accompanied her home to Bethlehem. Devoted to her mother-in-law. Married local landowner, Boaz.

**Samson** Phenomenally strong and fearless. He was betrayed by his wife, blinded and imprisoned by the Philistines in the time of the Judges.

**Samuel** Son of Hannah and Elkanah. Dedicated by his mother to God's service. Grew up with Eli, the priest at Shiloh. Judge and prophet who anointed Israel's first two kings.

**Sarah** Wife of Abraham. Mother of Isaac.

**Saul** First king of Israel. Failed to live up to expectations. Suffered extreme jealousy and deep depression. Killed in battle against the Philistines.

**Saul** *See* **Paul**.

**Shadrach** *See* **Abednego**.

**Silas** Accompanied Paul on missionary journey.

**Simeon** One of Joseph's brothers. Kept as a hostage to make sure the other brothers returned to Egypt with Benjamin.

**Simon Peter** *See* **Peter**.

**Simon** A Pharisee who invited Jesus to dinner and was horrified when a woman with a bad reputation anointed Jesus' feet with perfume.

**Sisera** Commander of King Jabin of Hazor's army. Killed by Jael when on the run after his army was defeated.

**Solomon** David's son, succeeded him as King of Israel. Built the Temple in Jerusalem. Had a reputation for wisdom.

**Stephen** Stoned to death. The first Christian martyr.

**Thomas** One of the twelve disciples. Didn't believe Jesus had risen until he saw and touched him.

**Uriah** Officer in David's army. Married to Bathsheba. David arranged for him to be killed so he could marry Bathsheba.

**Vashti** Married to Xerxes. Queen of Persia until Xerxes stripped her of her title and replaced her with Esther.

**Xerxes** King of Persia. Enjoyed socializing. Married to Vashti until she disobeyed him. Later married Esther.

**Zacchaeus** Chief tax collector in Jericho who climbed a tree to see Jesus.

**Zechariah** A priest, married to Elizabeth. Father of John the Baptist.

**Zedekiah** Replaced Jehoiakim as king. Refused to pay tribute to the Babylonians.

# THE END